THE TRAVEL SURVIVAL GUIDE

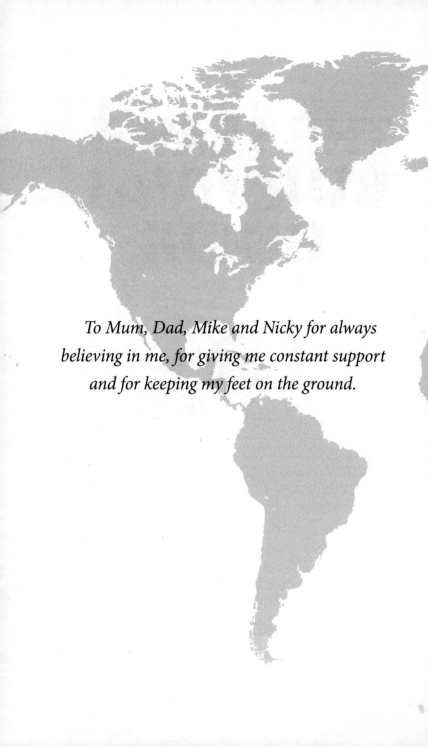

*To Mum, Dad, Mike and Nicky for always
believing in me, for giving me constant support
and for keeping my feet on the ground.*

THE TRAVEL SURVIVAL GUIDE

GET SMART
STAY SAFE

LLOYD FIGGINS

PORTICO

LLOYD FIGGINS

Lloyd Figgins is a former police officer, soldier and expedition leader. He is the founder and CEO of LFL Global Risk Mitigation and has worked in over 80 countries, including some of the most remote and hostile regions of the world. Lloyd is also Chairman of the Travel Risk & Incident Prevention (TRIP™) Group, which proactively seeks solutions to the safety challenges faced by travellers.

Lloyd is a Fellow of the Royal Geographical Society and a respected speaker on the subject of risk and crisis management. He often provides commentary in the media and makes regular appearances on the BBC, Fox News, ITV and Sky News.

www.lloydfiggins.com Risk Expert, Author, Speaker.
www.lflglobalrisk.com Protecting People, Assets and Reputations.
www.thetripgroup.com Working Together to Protect Travellers.
🐦 @LloydFiggins

CONTENTS

FOREWORD

by Sir Ranulph Fiennes

Overseas travel is often looked upon as glamorous but it can also be fraught with danger. Whether you're travelling on holiday or on business, or taking part in a major expedition, risk is part of the experience. If you don't put measures in place to mitigate those risks, things can and will go wrong.

My own expeditions have always placed a strong emphasis on risk management, from the logistics and planning phases all the way through to team selection and emergency evacuation plans. Not to do so would be remiss at best and negligent at worst. There are many accounts of those who haven't taken risk seriously and have paid the price.

In this book Lloyd recounts some of his adventures and provides some very useful safety advice to assist the traveller in making informed choices and decisions. He has been honest and transparent in terms of where he made mistakes, and he shares with the reader the lessons learnt from each experience.

Lloyd's approach to risk mitigation is practical, effective and backed up by his police, military and expedition-leading experience. In fact, there are few people who have the expertise and experience Lloyd has gained through travelling to over 80 countries and working in some of the world's more volatile regions, and it is these experiences which qualify him to write this excellent book.

CHAPTER ONE

LOOKING FOR LEMONS

Travel is wonderful. I can't think of anything better than exploring a new country or region. I believe that travel expands more than just the mind; it opens your soul to the wonders of this planet. My intention in writing this book is to encourage people to have the confidence to go out and discover the world and all it has to offer. However, it is important to do so safely and, of course, responsibly, in order to preserve our planet for future generations to enjoy.

My views on risk have been cultivated through my travels to more than 80 countries and the numerous experiences I've had, not all of them good. What I have learnt (sometimes the hard way) is that, if you ignore the warning signs, things can go wrong – and go very wrong, very quickly. And as with so many things in life, when you don't act upon the small risks, they can quickly escalate into bigger problems that you are just not equipped to handle. My number one rule of risk management is: never push a bad position; it's much more likely to get worse than to get better. So it's important to act while you still can and while you have a degree of control over your situation.

Therefore, the best way to avoid a poor situation is to do your research and prepare thoroughly for your trip. When travelling, a little knowledge is not just a good thing: it is potentially a lifesaver, so the more knowledge you have, the better able you are to deal with the hazards that come your way. I believe that preparation for a trip should be an exciting and enjoyable part of the overall travel experience.

The purpose of this book is to show you that by using careful planning and forethought, as well as tried and tested safety and security techniques, you can dramatically improve your chances of having trouble-free travel experiences on every trip you take. I also believe travel is, and should be, a hugely rewarding experience, and what I would like to do is to help you learn how to recognise travel risks and then to mitigate them effectively.

Understanding the basic rules of travel is more important today than ever. I'm not alone in my constant desire for the freedom, adventure and stimulation of international exploration. Travel and tourism form one of the world's largest industries, with an economy valued at £1.43 trillion (US$2.2 trillion) and growing. In the past 60 years, the number of people travelling from one country to another has increased exponentially. In 1955, just 45 million people moved from one country to another. Today, thanks to extensive air travel routes and higher disposable incomes, just over a billion people are exploring new places around the globe every year.

Over this period the nature of the travel industry has changed irrevocably. No longer are we limited to the suggestions of a helpful assistant at our local high-street travel agency. Thanks to the wonders of technology, we can 'pre-explore' all sorts of exciting and exotic destinations before we make our own carefully researched choices.

The current travel trend is dominated by 'interesting' or 'adventure' holidays, which may or may not involve going off the beaten track. Gap years, where both young and more mature travellers disappear for months at a time to places many of their friends have barely heard of, are also hugely popular. It seems that these adventures have become a rite of passage for a lot of people today. Meanwhile, as business becomes ever more global, executives can find themselves being sent out to far-flung corners of the world at a moment's notice. There is no denying it: travel dominates all of our lives in one way or another.

But while the world is undoubtedly more accessible than it was, it doesn't necessarily follow that it is safer. Anyone with even half an eye on international current affairs will be very aware that the opposite is the case. In July 2017, the UK's Foreign & Commonwealth Office (FCO) advised against travel to all or part of more than 50 nation states around the world. The vast majority were in Africa and the Middle East, with terrorism, kidnap and disease cited as the main threats.

None of this is to say that you should give up on your dreams of international adventure and stay at home. Far from it. It is extremely unlikely that anything bad will happen to you (particularly if you prepare well). To put this into perspective, the odds of your being killed by a terrorist overseas are one in 20 million. Your chances of being struck by lightning, however, are one in 600,000.

I've been teaching risk and crisis management all over the world for many years and my knowledge has been gained from direct experience. All of the incidents recorded in this book actually happened to me. I've learnt many lessons on my travels and am now able to share them, in the hope of preventing others from finding out the hard way what can go wrong.

***

It was a cool, still summer evening in Northern British Columbia. The water on the lake was clear and glassy and the gently swaying Douglas firs around its edge were perfectly reflected in the smooth surface. The only sounds that could be heard were the soft paddle strokes as our canoes nosed their way over the water. Everyone on board was acutely aware that we were edging towards the end of a nine-day trip, and our first cold beer was tantalisingly close. We could almost taste it.

It was not far now. The cedar deck was fast approaching and, with it, the promise of hot showers and maybe a soft mattress. In what seemed like no time at all our party of four was sitting on terra firma at the small lakeside lodge. In reality the lodge was pretty ramshackle, but to us at that moment it was a gilded palace. We all had broad post-trip smiles and were enjoying the setting as much as the eagerly anticipated refreshments.

'You have an amazing place here,' I said to the lodge owner, nodding at the picture-book view. 'The lake is so beautiful and peaceful.'

The woman stared out to the lake and a sad smile crept across her face.

'It's not always like this,' she said slowly. Tearing her gaze from the placid waters, she turned to face me. 'That's where, last year, two people had their lemons come up.'

I frowned and glanced around the group. The others had stopped talking and were focused on our conversation. We all looked perplexed.

'How do you mean, "their lemons come up"?' I asked.

She paused for a moment and then took a deep breath.

'Well, life is like a one-armed bandit slot machine,' she began. 'If four lemons come up, you're out.'

I looked at my group: no, clearly they didn't understand either.

'Sorry to be slow on the uptake, but could you explain?' I pressed.

She nodded and paused again, clearly weighing up the best way to put it.

'Life's about looking out for lemons,' she said at last. 'Each lemon is a hazard, and unless a hazard gets sorted, it can be a problem. If you get four of them in a line, like you do on a slot machine, it's not looking good. The people last year had all their lemons lined up.'

Everyone was silent.

'To begin with,' she continued, 'they were novices and not confident swimmers. So that was lemon one.' She started to count on her fingers.

'Next, they were not wearing buoyancy aids: lemon two.

'They ignored all the advice and were out paddling in the middle of the lake. That was lemon three.

'This all happened at 5:30 in the afternoon, just as it was starting to get dark. The wind picked up and they capsized. That was lemon four,' she said, holding up a fourth finger. 'Four lemons, and sadly they died.'

For a few moments no one was quite sure what to say.

'So looking for lemons is like doing a risk assessment – looking for potential hazards and what can go wrong?' I asked.

'You can call it what you like but it's common sense,' she said with a shrug. 'We just talk about looking out for lemons.'

***

In a lot of cases, a good healthy dose of common sense is the key to avoiding unwanted incidents and I'd like to share a couple of stories from my childhood that demonstrate that not all of us are born with common sense. Especially me, it would seem. However, we do all have the opportunity to hone our skills so that we can protect ourselves and others in the most challenging of situations, and in this book I will outline the know-how you need to do just that.

But first to those stories. I spent my earliest years in Singapore. We were a military family and my father was posted to the Far East when I was just 8 months old. In those days, Singapore was a world away from the UK, and not just geographically. It was also a far cry from the bustling, modern and thriving city it is today. Much of Singapore was still surrounded by jungle and most people still got around by rickshaw or bicycle. The heat was profoundly oppressive and it felt like you could never get dry. I was always wet, largely because I was always in the sea or a swimming pool, trying to stay cool.

Despite the discomforts, I was something of a minor celebrity in Singapore, as a baby and later as a toddler. The reason being, I had the most brilliant head of blond hair, and when we travelled on buses local people clamoured to touch my head for good luck. My mum and I never had to wait in a queue or stand on a bus, as the locals would always give up their seats for the little blond child and his mother.

My older brother, Mike, being dark haired, was not extended such privileges. Perhaps this goes some way to explaining why, following my arrival in the Figgins family, Mike dedicated his early life to getting me into trouble. In fact it's incredible that we get on so well nowadays, given some of the mischief he got me into.

The first married-quarters accommodation my parents were offered was far from ideal. It was infested with cockroaches the size of large mice, as well as spiders and lizards that clearly had no fear of humans. Outside in the yard, snakes were regular visitors, and my mum recalls watching a python casually winding its way through a tree as she was waiting for a bus. Inside the house was no better: the furniture supplied by the Royal Air Force (RAF) was old and there were rusty nails protruding from both my cot and my brother's bed.

Mike and I were oblivious to our surroundings and actually quite enjoyed our Singapore home. We would run around the garden half-naked and have all sorts of adventures. I started to develop an unhealthy interest in storm drains and the creatures, especially the millipedes, that resided in them. In fact, they became an important part of my diet, until my parents caught me tucking into a particularly large specimen.

One thing they couldn't do was stop me from exploring, and this proved a constant worry to them, particularly as I grew older and roamed further afield. They would invariably find me in some corner playing with whatever wildlife came to hand, and in Singapore there were plenty of options.

My 'expeditions' became ever more adventurous and I became ever better at avoiding re-capture. Storm drains were still a favourite, but by then I was starting to realise that the creatures they hosted were just the hors d'oeuvres and that there were much bigger opportunities to be had outside the garden perimeter. Despite my parents' attempts to 'Lloyd proof' the garden, I'd often find ways to escape and taste the true potential of the outside world.

Spring of 1969 saw the Figgins family take a trip to the local zoo. The animals and other attractions fascinated me. Now, zoos in the 1960s were primitive and crowded places, with little regard for safety. This undoubtedly played into the hands of my mischievous older brother.

When we arrived at the crocodile enclosure, the other visitors were engaged in a game of throwing loose change at the poor creatures, presumably in an attempt to get them to move. That the attempts were clearly futile didn't seem to deter them. The activity seemed to be something of a daily tradition, judging by the ample piles of money littered all over the ground.

'Those coins would make us rich,' Mike whispered in my ear. 'You just need to slip though these bars.'

I looked at him wide-eyed. Although still a toddler, I was wise enough to know that his by now regular schemes didn't always bode well for me.

'I'd do it myself but I can't fit through,' he said with a nonchalant shrug. 'The family needs the money and Mum and Dad will be really proud of you...'

There was a huge gasp from the crowd as they saw the small blond kid squeeze through the railings and toddle towards the collection of coins.

On hearing the commotion, my parents immediately looked at one another and asked in unison, 'Where's Lloyd?'

Their question was soon answered by the large crowd that had surged forward to the elevated platform above the crocodile enclosure. To their horror my parents saw their younger child inside the enclosure and heading purposefully towards the water where a number of crocs were bathing.

I was actually making pretty good progress when a local chap recognised the seriousness of the situation and jumped the fence to remove the potential meal from the now very attentive crocs.

My parents were mortified and more than a little embarrassed, not only that they had failed to prevent my initial escape but also that they now had to come forward in front of the large crowd and claim this renegade child as their own flesh and blood. For my part, I was more than a little miffed at having been manhandled by a complete stranger just yards from my goal.

The family day out was abandoned and we headed for the exit and home, but not before Mike dared me to poke a monkey in a cage. The primate bit me for my trouble. (To this day Mike continues to deny he had anything to do with this and many other incidents.)

So there you go, no common sense. Worse still, I didn't even learn the valuable lesson that I should clearly ignore everything my brother said.

Which brings me to the second story.

By the time I was nine, the family had moved to Cyprus. Mike's dares continued, the incentives invariably starting with something along the lines of: 'No one has ever done this, Lloyd. If you do it, you will be the first person in the world to do it… ever.'

At this stage I still believed anything and everything my brother told me.

One day, Mike came to me very excitedly. He had heard of a challenge that no one had ever completed and wanted to know whether I was interested in being the first person to do it. I would have been wise to say no, but I didn't learn to do that until many years later.

The never before achieved challenge centred around a hill in a defunct corner of the RAF Akrotiri base. At the top of this hill was an old building. No one could remember what the building had been used for, but the road leading up to it was known locally as Devil's Hill and was the steepest I had ever seen. The road was closed to traffic (although, in fairness, there weren't many cars in our neighbourhood that would have been capable of getting up it) and Mike's plan was for me to be the first person to cycle down it. Somehow he managed to convince me that this was a sure-fire ticket to local stardom.

Word soon got round that the younger Figgins boy was going to attempt to cycle down Devil's Hill. A group of children gathered and rode their bikes to the foot of the hill. (I couldn't help but notice they all had far better bikes than mine.) They surrounded Mike and me in awed silence as we all stood looking up at my challenge. From that angle it was more apparent than ever that this was a very steep hill indeed. Most of the children decided that it was too dangerous to even walk up to the summit and opted to wait at the bottom.

There were clear warning signs saying 'no entry'. Mike and I steered our way around them and started pushing our bikes up the hill in the searing summer heat. It was hard going, especially since the tarmac had seen better days and in some places had crumbled completely. We were dressed in our usual attire of shorts and flip-flops. We rarely wore anything else, certainly never t-shirts.

When we reached the halfway point, Mike threw his bike down on the verge and himself down beside it.

'I'll wait here to get the best view of you whizzing past,' he said, settling down and nonchalantly plucking a stalk of dried grass to chew. 'Now come on, everyone's waiting.'

I took a deep breath and stared at the summit before plodding on.

'Make sure you pedal hard to start with, and then just hold on,' was Mike's parting advice.

Thanks bro, I thought as I struggled on, pushing my bike.

When I finally got to the top, I peered back down towards the bottom. The large group of expectant boys looked so small I could barely see them. I could just about make out Mike at the halfway point, standing upright now and impatiently waving me on.

I tried to compose myself and straddled my bike. My heart was thumping and I felt a little light-headed. To calm myself down I gave the brakes a quick squeeze to test them. They seemed fine.

With my feet firmly planted on the crumbling road, I stole another glance down the course. There was no escaping it, this was a bloody steep hill and very scary.

Mike's waving was getting even more impatient now, and I became vaguely aware that he was shouting at the top of his voice, although it was hard to make out exactly what he was saying: his words were stolen away by the light breeze that wafted over the top of the hill. I looked beyond him to the mob below, and could just about make out that they were waving too. There was no way I could back out now.

Taking a deep breath, I lifted my feet on to the pedals and started pedalling as hard as I could, just as Mike had told me. Within a few seconds, though, my pedals were spinning around at a tremendous rate, far faster than my legs could ever move. I instantly realised that Mike's advice was stupid: there was no need to pedal at all on a gradient so steep, doubly so since my bike had no gears. My only option was just to hang on for dear life. I had never gone this fast on a bike before and after the initial shock had died down it was briefly quite exhilarating.

I was fast approaching Mike's position when everything seemed to go into slow motion.

To begin with, the handlebars began to move from side to side, but the front wheel didn't change direction correspondingly. The handlebars had clearly become loose, which meant I no longer had control of my bike. Fighting the rising feeling of panic, I tried the brakes. Nothing. They clearly weren't designed to cope with such speeds. I'd had it. I just knew it. In a final violent act – which felt like it lasted forever yet was over in a few seconds – the bike lurched from side to side before bucking, as the front wheel turned 90 degrees on itself.

In an instant I was flying through the air.

I hit the tarmac at what felt like terminal velocity and skidded past Mike on my chest. I can still see the look of horror on his face as the skin was torn from my body. My brother had to get on his own bike to reach the place where I ended up, about 25 yards (23m) away.

'Are you all right?' he asked, sounding genuinely shocked.

I looked at him, then looked at my bike, and managed to say, 'Yes, I think so.'

The other boys rushed up the hill to join us. One of them picked up my bike while, shaking slightly, I got to my feet. There were murmurs of amazement and approval that I was still in one piece.

I didn't share the general confidence. Indeed, as I looked down at my lacerated body, it was pretty obvious to me that I needed to get help. The fall had torn the skin off my knees, chest, back and one arm. It had all literally gone.

The boy looking after my bike had pulled out a tool kit and tightened the nut on the handlebars.

'There you go, Figgins, that should work now,' he said confidently.

The thought flitted across my mind that maybe it would have been wise to have done that maintenance before I began my descent. As we set off down the hill these thoughts were pushed to the back of my mind by the agonising bursts of pain that had begun to surge through my body.

'I think it might be a good idea to head off home,' I said to Mike.

'Nah, you go if you want to,' he said with a dismissive sweep of his hand. 'I'm staying out here with this lot.'

There was no compassion, no concern that his ridiculous scheme had nearly killed me, although I'm not quite sure what I expected. All I could do was to jump back on my bike and start the ride home.

It was then that the pain really kicked in. The light wind ripped into my open wounds like a thousand red-hot daggers. The faster I tried to cycle, the worse it got. I knew I was in trouble. The wounds were bleeding quite badly now and the tears started to flow.

When I reached our house I realised I was locked out. My mum and dad were still at work and wouldn't be home for at least an hour. I dumped my bike in the street and ran next door, screaming in pain. The neighbour, who had heard my wails, came running out and as soon as he saw me realised it was serious. He grabbed his car keys with one hand and me with the other, and told his daughter to tell my mum and dad when they returned that he had taken me to the medical centre.

On arrival at the base medical facility, a doctor and nurse immediately came to my aid, and that's when the agony really started. The nurse was given the unenviable task of cleaning the wounds, but this proved difficult since half of Devil's Hill was still imbedded in my body, and some of it quite deeply. She plucked away with tweezers, trying to get out what she could, but she didn't have much success.

The doctor came along and said (somewhat cavalierly in my view), 'Stick him in the shower and we'll jet-wash the dirt out.'

The pain of the jets of water hitting my exposed wounds was worse than anything I had ever experienced. I struggled but was held down by the medical staff until they had got the majority of the debris out of my body. Then it was back to the nurse, who continued to systematically pluck at the more stubborn bits of road still stuck in me.

As if that was not enough of an ordeal, then came the iodine, which took pain to a whole new level. The only way I could get through it was to focus on that stupid brother of mine and his absurd dare that had got me into this. I swore I would never speak to him again. It obviously escaped my attention that it had been my choice to actually go through with the challenge.

It was not over yet, either. My dad arrived just as the medical staff decided that, to complete their torture, they would put me in a salt bath. Pain screamed from every piece of exposed flesh, all at the same time. I was no longer capable of making a sound. Tears flowed down my cheeks as I looked desperately into my father's eyes, silently begging him to make the pain stop. But there was nothing he could do.

Eventually, they managed to clean my wounds to the satisfaction of the doctor, and they dressed them and sent me home. I had a salt bath three times a day for the next two weeks and my dressings were changed every day. It put a temporary halt to my exploits, and for once Mike seemed to register the magnitude of what had happened to me.

This incident and others that followed (for, yes, there were more) didn't stop him from using me as his proxy for years to come. I did, however, gradually learn to take better care of myself. Most importantly, I realised that if I was going to survive I would have to get better at recognising and mitigating risk.

My early choice of a career in the police, which I joined shortly after leaving school, was hugely beneficial to me in this respect. Here I was confronted by a range of risks in all their different forms and was taught how to effectively manage dangerous situations. My police career exposed me to the sorts of things that most people just don't get to see, and it set me on a path that in many ways I'm still following today.

After leaving the police I spent some time travelling, and when I returned to the UK I joined the British Army. My spell in the armed forces gave me the dual benefit of continuing my education in risk management while also allowing me to follow my passion for adventure. The Army actively encourages its soldiers to pursue adventurous activities – and the best bit is that you get paid to do some pretty amazing things.

Moreover, the Army paid me to get many useful qualifications, some of which allowed me to become an expedition leader when I left government service. I had long since recognised that I enjoyed nothing more than exploring the world but I had learnt through experience that it was an expensive hobby. Therefore, if I could find a way to get paid to travel, that would surely be the ultimate job.

Through the military I became qualified as a mountain leader and I also became a wilderness emergency medical technician (W-EMT). This qualification allowed me to join expeditions as a medic and made me a more attractive proposition to expedition companies, since I could take the dual role of leader and medic. As part of my medical training, I spent time working with my local ambulance service as a first responder, and this (along with my experiences on expeditions) exposed me to a wide range of medical situations.

After years of leading expeditions all over the globe, I found myself taking on work specifically involving risk management, safety and security – basically, creating strategies to make travel safer. The combination of my police, military and expedition work turned out to be a winning formula and I have written various manuals and field-safety guides, many of which have been translated into different languages.

The development of my career coincided with a recognition, particularly in the corporate world, that it is not enough to stick executives on a plane and hope for the best. Companies have had to develop cohesive risk-management plans as a priority and have turned to experienced consultants, like me, to protect their teams. I have worked with organisations from all sorts of industries including oil and gas, mining, tourism, scientific research, higher education and conservation, as well as one or two overseas governments.

These days I am the founder and CEO of LFL Global Risk Mitigation, which specialises in keeping people safe when travelling overseas. I've spent much of my professional life in the more remote and hostile environments of our planet where I've seen risks of every kind. My company provides tools that identify and mitigate hazards, as well as creating emergency response and evacuation plans in case things go wrong.

Those who remember the reckless young lad who would do anything for a challenge often accuse me of being a poacher turned gamekeeper, and in many ways I see this as a compliment. No one could say that I have been risk-averse in my life. By the same token, it's that exposure to danger that has allowed me to make informed judgements on how best to mitigate risk for others.

It would be very simple as an international risk specialist to simply say 'no' to anything that looks remotely dangerous, but that's not effective risk management. I prefer to look at the ways in which people *can* do things rather than for reasons why they can't. I am only able to do this because of what I have seen and experienced myself. I then apply those successful risk-mitigation methodologies to suit the requirements of my clients.

Even after all my travels, I am still a firm believer that the world is out there to be discovered. I refuse to listen to the naysayers who declare that they won't travel here or there because it isn't safe. As long as you prepare well, get the requisite training, acknowledge the pitfalls and use your common sense, odds on you'll be fine.

I have also stopped listening to my brother.

CHAPTER TWO

AIRCRAFT SAFETY

For many of us, the real adventure begins once we set foot on board the aircraft that will take us to our chosen destination. For others, though, this aspect of the trip is all of their worst nightmares rolled into one – and then some. Fear of flying is one of the most common phobias. Statistically speaking, in every row of three seats on a commercial airliner there is at least one passenger who would really rather be elsewhere.

If you count yourself as the one in that row of three, let's start with the basics. On average, you'd need to be strapped into that seat every day for 19,000 years to be involved in a serious accident. The chances of dying on any given flight with a major airline are just one in 4.7 million. The probability of your being killed in a traffic accident, on the other hand, is one in 14,000. In fact, you are more likely to be struck by lightning than to die on your flight. The most dangerous part of your trip is probably the drive to the airport.

Things are getting better all the time, too. In the 1970s, on average 68 commercial planes crashed each year, causing 1,676 fatalities. Advances in cockpit and navigation technology, as well as improvements in the aircraft themselves, have seen those figures almost halve, to 40 crashes and 832 deaths in 2014. In the same year, 100,000 flights took off around the globe every day and, out of

33 million annual flights, only 21 crashed. It's a pretty impressive safety record.

And the global crash rate is only as high as it is because much of the developing world is far behind the west in terms of safety. Aircraft in these developing countries are often older, flown by less experienced pilots, to less stringent flight regulations. Similarly, major carriers also tend to have a better safety record than smaller ones, because they can afford to hire the best and most experienced staff. Human error is the principal cause of 80 per cent of crashes.

While the chances of there being complications are remote, there are also things you can do to considerably improve your odds. This chapter will show you how to steer clear of potential problems and demonstrate what you can do to improve your chances of survival, should you find yourself in one of those extremely rare emergency situations.

MY STORY

In early 1999, I found myself flying from Lima in Peru to Bogotá in Colombia. The trip was partly business and partly for my own exploration. I was due to meet up with my good friend Maverick. I'd nicknamed him Maverick shortly after we first met, because he had trained as a helicopter pilot and the only famous pilot I could think of at the time was the Tom Cruise character from the movie *Top Gun*. It was either that or Biggles and he didn't look like a Biggles to me. We had travelled extensively in Southeast Asia and he was the ideal companion for this Colombian trip.

The business element of the visit was to research a route for a potential new expedition in the foothills of the Sierra Nevada de Santa Marta mountains in the north of the country.

At the time, Colombia was a country still very much at war with itself. The conflict between the government and the

Revolutionary Armed Forces of Colombia (FARC) had resulted in most western governments advising against travel to many parts of the country. Crime rates were off the scale, life was cheap and kidnappings were commonplace.

During the three-hour flight I was preoccupied with contemplating the various safety risks and going over my security and contingency planning, when the aircraft started behaving in a fashion I was not entirely familiar or, indeed, comfortable with.

We had flown into a storm, and at first it felt like the regular turbulence you get on most flights. Having flown regularly in Latin America, I thought nothing of it. But then, around half an hour ahead of our intended landing time, things got distinctly worse.

I looked out the window. One minute the wing was as high as it could be without the aircraft inverting; the next instant it was as low as it was possible to go without the aircraft flipping over. I was sitting towards the back of the aircraft, which in those days was the smoking area. My position afforded me a view down the length of the plane and it wasn't a pretty sight.

The scene inside reflected the erratic movement I could see through the window: everything was being tossed from side to side and from back to front. The seat belt signs had been on for a while, but I could see people now trying frantically to tighten their belts as much as they could, and I joined them in this act of self-preservation. As I looked about the cabin, I could see expressions of deep concern etched on every face. With every passing minute the turbulence was getting worse, and it felt like the aircraft was quite literally being thrown around the sky by some giant hand.

The in-flight map showing our route indicated that we were flying at 2,000 feet (600m), and every few moments I got an alarming glimpse through the clouds of the ground below. Then seconds later, all I could see were the dark clouds of the storm above us as the plane lurched the other way.

Some passengers were throwing up, while others screamed in terror. The engines of the aircraft were screaming too. Each time we were tossed about the sky it felt as though the engines were being pushed to their limits, and they screeched like an animal in pain. Glancing behind, I saw that the cabin crew were strapped firmly into their seats and had turned a ghostly shade of white. These women, who were always so calm and reassuring, were terrified and, like many other passengers, were praying and crossing themselves over and over again.

At least they had a god to turn to. I had decided long ago that I didn't believe in God, although he seemed to be pretty bloody omnipotent at that moment, as something all-powerful tossed the plane across the Colombian skies.

As I looked down the cabin again, I wondered whether it could get any worse. The screaming, praying and vomiting had reached fever pitch and even those who had remained calm up until now were joining in. It was a scene of pure panic, and panic can be quite contagious.

But for some reason, I felt like an observer, detached from the reality of what was going on around me. My thought processes were clear. Through the clouds I could see the earth getting closer and the wings moving from extremely high to extremely low. Nevertheless, I decided if we had survived this long (about 15 minutes of severe turbulence), we could make it to the airport.

Then everything went quiet. The screaming and the heaves of those vomiting stopped, and even the engines seemed eerily soundless. It was as if someone had snapped off the volume.

What was obvious now, however, was the number of articles floating about the cabin. In fact, anything not secured was simply suspended in thin air. The ashtrays from the seat arms were hovering next to me at eye level and there was a bottle of Johnnie Walker Black Label (not mine) floating perilously close to my head. The hair of the woman in the seat in front of me rose from her head like a fan, and everything seemed to be happening in slow motion.

It was in that instant that it dawned on me: we were falling, quite simply falling out of the sky.

I had always wanted to experience zero gravity, but not like this. Was this how it was going to end? An airline fatality? At least people would remember how I had died, and it was certainly more spectacular than boring old natural causes. I was disappointed that my life might be coming to an end, as I still had so much that I wanted to see and do. Surprisingly quickly, however, I resigned myself to my circumstances and accepted that in all probability this trip was not going to end well.

I could tell that I wasn't the only one thinking like this. The cabin seemed almost at peace; the earlier panic seemed to have evaporated, replaced by an atmosphere of near tranquillity.

The calm didn't last long, however, and when we re-equalised it was with an almighty thud. We were thankfully still airborne and oxygen masks dropped down in front of us, but no one, including me, reached for them.

The noise in the cabin before the fall was nothing compared to the noise now. The screaming became hysterical and ear-piercing, and people were in tears as they prayed, convinced that they would soon be meeting the very entity they were praying to.

I looked out of the window and could see that the ground was really quite close, probably no more than 600 feet (180m) away. The wings, however, were still doing their crazy dance. Another drop would probably see the end of us.

To my side there was a young woman, the only other European on the flight, and she was no longer screaming or vomiting; she was simply shaking and staring blankly in my direction. I doubt she could even see me. Tears streamed down her face, and I knew I was looking into the eyes of fear itself. I called out to her above the uproar, telling her that we were nearly on the ground and that in a few minutes it would all be over and we would be safe. The problem was that, in this situation, minutes seemed like hours.

She had clearly been sick, so I reached into my pocket and pulled out a stick of chewing gum. As I passed her the gum, she looked at me and grabbed my hand. I had never seen anyone look so utterly vulnerable or afraid in my life, and she held on to my hand as though she was holding on to life itself.

'Where are you from?' I asked, trying to sound as calm and as reassuring as I could above the din of the cabin and the scream of the engines.

'Holland,' came the choked response.

'Well, we are going to get out of this,' I said and made to pull away, but she wouldn't let me go.

'Please hold my hand. I don't want to die alone,' she sobbed.

'No one's going to die. We're going to get to the ground and off this plane very soon.'

There was no way she was letting go of my hand. For the remainder of the flight I kept talking to her. And even after we eventually landed and were bumping along the runway, I carried on talking. I have no idea what I said but by the time we had come to a standstill I had managed to get her to smile.

As I left the aircraft, the captain appeared from the cockpit. He looked slightly sweaty but relieved.

'So how far did we drop?' I asked.

He looked at me and quietly replied, 'Two hundred feet.'

I thanked him and made a mental note to check the weather forecast before I flew back to Lima.

IMPROVING THE ODDS

Nowadays, I am very particular about the airlines I choose to fly on and I always check their safety records before booking a seat, particularly when it comes to the smaller carriers in the more remote parts of the world. You don't need to be an airline industry expert to do this and there are plenty of resources in the public domain that can provide sound advice on which airlines meet European and US safety standards and, more importantly, which do not. Of these resources, the Aviation Safety Network (www. aviation-safety.net) probably offers the most comprehensive database of incidents and airline safety records.

Looking at the lists of airlines banned from flying into the European Union or the United States is a useful indication of problematic carriers. Some countries, in fact, have such poor aviation records that none of their airlines meet EU standards. This is something you should definitely bear in mind if you are travelling to one of these countries. If you need to use such an airline, you will also need to check with your insurance company whether this affects or, indeed, invalidates your travel insurance.

In an era when you can often pre-book seats online, anything which will give you an edge in surviving a potential crash has got to be worth exploring. One of the questions I am often asked is, 'Where are the safest seats on an aircraft?' If you listen to airlines they will tell you that one seat is as safe as another. However, this is not borne out by research carried out by *Popular Mechanics* magazine, which has examined data from every commercial air crash in the United States since 1971. Their research clearly shows that sitting at the back of a plane is safer than sitting in the mid-section, and certainly safer than sitting towards the front.

In fact, the survival rate in first-class and business-class cabins is only 49 per cent, compared to 56 per cent in the sections forward and over the wings. But by far the safest area is the back of the plane, where survival rates rise to 69 per cent.

It is also widely recognised that your chances of survival decrease the further you get away from an emergency exit; and decrease dramatically if you are more than five rows away from an exit. Thick smoke and fire are major hazards during crashes so, just as a precaution, it's always wise to count the number of rows between you and the nearest exit as soon as you get on the aircraft. Aisle seats are going to allow you a quicker escape than window seats: if you're leaving in a hurry, you don't want to have to climb over a couple of other passengers on your way out.

In years gone by, I always used to try and get the window seat in an emergency exit row itself, believing that this not only gave me the best chance of survival but also provided a bit of extra legroom. That's fine until you take into account that the wings of an aircraft are full of highly combustible fuel. Added to that, when planes are hijacked, the hijackers invariably occupy the emergency exit and bulkhead rows, and when the plane is on the tarmac, stand in the open doorways to keep an eye out for rescue forces approaching the aircraft.

Always listen carefully to the in-flight briefing. Every time I fly I hear the crew urging passengers to listen to the short presentation, even if they are frequent flyers, yet when I look around most people are engrossed in choosing their in-flight entertainment or chatting amongst themselves.

These people are really missing out. There's a good reason why airlines keep telling us to wear our seat belts and how to fasten and release them. In crashes, there is a lot of panic and people automatically revert to learnt behaviour. This usually means that they attempt to undo their seat belt as if it were the one in their car – which it is not. This has often been the difference between those who have made it off an aircraft in an emergency and those who have not.

My experience on the Lima-Bogotá flight taught me that, despite advances in technology and safety measures, we are still very vulnerable when we fly, and anything not strapped down will float and then crash to the floor of the cabin with tremendous force. This includes passengers.

WHAT TO DO IF IT ALL GOES WRONG

To research what actually happens in an aircraft emergency, I recently found myself on board an aircraft I knew was going to crash – a British Airways training simulator. The flight started just like any other. There were 23 passengers and three crew on board and we were given the usual safety demonstration as the aircraft taxied to the runway. The crew checked that our seat belts were correctly fastened, that our tray tables were stowed, our armrests were down and our seats in the upright position.

The captain gave us some information about the flight and then said, 'Cabin crew, seats for take-off.'

I heard the familiar increase in engine noise as the jet roared down the runway and then lifted into the air. There was a slight shaking as we left the ground but nothing I hadn't experienced on hundreds of previous flights.

Within a few minutes, though, things changed – and changed very quickly.

I first realised there was something wrong when one of the passengers shouted, 'Fire! There's a fire!'

I noticed that there was smoke in the cabin – and that it was getting thicker. Other passengers started looking around and hitting the call buttons above their heads. It was dawning on us all that we were in a metal tube that was rapidly filling with smoke.

A voice came over the PA: 'This is an emergency. Brace! Brace!'

We did as we were told, placing feet flat on the floor and leaning forward to rest our heads on the seat in front, with our hands around the back of our heads.

The crew continued shouting, 'Brace! Brace! Brace!'

One of the passengers must have looked up to see what was going on and the crew member reacted immediately.

'You, get your head down!' she shouted. 'Brace, brace!'

The aircraft was shaking, then it went very dark and I couldn't see a thing. We seemed to have got back down to the ground again.

The voice came back on the PA: 'This is an emergency. Evacuate! Evacuate!'

The emergency lighting was just about visible through the dense smoke. I couldn't see the crew – I could barely see the passenger in front of me – but I could hear them hollering at us, 'Unfasten your seat belts! Come this way!'

Before I knew it someone's hand was on my shoulder guiding me towards the exit. Another hand was on the top of my head and a voice was shouting, 'Jump!'

I was out.

The whole event had taken only a couple of minutes, from the time the smoke first appeared, through the emergency landing, to getting out of the aircraft. There had been no time to think: it was simply a question of survival.

Being in a training simulator, we were obviously expecting something to happen before we entered the cabin but that didn't really diminish the urgency of the situation, which set the scene for a day of training with British Airways' flight safety experts. Between them the training team have countless flying hours under their belts. They are the best in the business at instructing regular travellers on what happens in an emergency and how you need to react in order to improve your chances of getting out alive.

The message that came across loud and strong was: pay attention to the safety briefing, read the aircraft safety card and listen to the instructions of the cabin crew.

The course also taught skills that most people don't ordinarily get a chance to practise, such as how to open the doors of an aircraft in an emergency. The front and rear doors are simple enough: you just need to follow the instructions and keep the momentum of the opening door swinging outwards.

However, the over-wing exits on smaller aircraft are not so straightforward. The first thing to know is that they weigh just under 20 kilos (44 pounds) and you need to open them while you are still in your seat. If you (or whoever is sitting in the emergency exit window seat) don't have the strength to lift that kind of weight whilst seated, you (or they) are in the wrong seat.

The next thing you need to know is that the door falls inwards, and if you don't get your head out of the way, you are going to get hit by 20 kilos of aircraft door. You should also warn the people seated next to you to sit back or they will get clobbered too. You then need to have the strength to throw the thing out of the aircraft so that you can get out yourself.

Of course, before you do any of this, you need to make sure it's safe to open any of the aircraft doors in the first place. Check that there's not a fire just outside the window, and remember to unfasten your seat belt before attempting to leave the aircraft. All of this might sound obvious but try doing it in an emergency situation, when there's smoke in the cabin, it's pitch black and people are screaming.

It's a widely known fact that smoke will kill you long before the fire gets to you, and a particularly fascinating part of the course was being taken into a 'smoke room', which is configured to look like an aircraft cabin. The thermostat is turned right up and smoke is released. The heat makes the smoke rise and if you're standing you can't see a thing. Down on the ground, though, the air is crystal clear. In a real emergency, keep down and follow the emergency lighting, and do so quickly but without panicking.

It's also helpful to know what to do during a cabin decompression incident. You will do yourself a huge favour if you ensure that your seat belt is always fastened while seated. If you need any incentive, it's worth pointing out that if you're not strapped in and something happens, you'll end up floating around the cabin at best, and outside the cabin at worst.

Moreover, if the oxygen masks drop, you need to get one on as soon as possible. If you don't, hypoxia will start to take effect after 15 seconds and you will be completely unconscious within 45 seconds. That's why you have to put your own mask on before assisting others with theirs.

If you are unfortunate enough to ditch on water, it is essential to know – beforehand – where your life jacket is and how to fit it properly.

Finally, get to know the right technique for jumping down emergency evacuation slides. As with most things in life, there's a right way and a wrong way. You don't want to get this wrong, particularly since on some of the larger aircraft it can be a long way down.

Hold on to your clothing (where the collar of a shirt sits is a good place) and sit up rather than lying down. When you get to the bottom of the slide, move away quickly or else the next person down the slide is going to plough into you at high speed. Most emergency evacuation slides double up as life rafts, so be sure to stay attached to the slide.

British Airways has taken the initiative in providing flight safety awareness courses for ordinary people and I would recommend these courses wholeheartedly. There can be little doubt that the more people are aware of what happens in an emergency, the greater everyone's chances of survival. Understanding how best to react to what the cabin crew are doing to manage an emergency is essential knowledge for anyone getting on an aircraft.

Hopefully you will now be more inclined to pay full attention to the safety briefing the next time you board a plane.

AIRCRAFT SAFETY CHECKLIST

- Always check the safety record of the airline you intend to fly with. If it doesn't have a good record, choose another, even if it costs a little more. How much is your life worth to you?
- Where possible, pre-book your seat. Statistically, the rear of the aircraft is safer and aisle seats will allow you to get out quicker.
- Never sit in a row more than five rows away from an emergency exit and always count the number of seat rows between you and the nearest exit.

- Familiarise yourself with your nearest emergency exit and visualise how you would get there in an emergency (bearing in mind that there will be general panic and other people clambering to reach it as well).
- Do not remove your shoes before take-off. If you need to get off the aircraft quickly or if there's a fire, you will be glad of your shoes. Remember also to have them on for landing. Most incidents happen at take-off or landing. Avoid travelling in high-heeled shoes.
- Read the safety card and watch the crew's safety demonstration.
- Practise fastening and unfastening your seat belt a few times before take-off. Get used to how the seat belt works and feels.
- Check to see that your life jacket is stowed where it should be. If it's not there, ask for one. Airlines tend to carry spares.
- If you are flying in a light aircraft, chartering an aircraft or doing bush flying, remember that safety records are poorer in mountainous areas, and also in Africa and Russia. Fly in daylight and in good weather, and don't pressure aircrew to fly against their better judgement. Again, check the safety record of the company you're thinking of flying with.
- Have a small torch with you. An LED head torch in particular is very useful when travelling.
- In an emergency evacuation, leave all personal belongings behind. Carry-on bags will slow your exit and create a hazard for you and others.
- Don't wait for others to move: many will be paralysed by fear. Get yourself out regardless of what others are doing.
- During an emergency or crash landing, the cabin filling with smoke is one of the great dangers. You can be quickly disabled by smoke, so get down low and try to get out fast.
- Listen to the instructions of the cabin crew and follow their commands. Their purpose is to protect you.

A FEW WORDS ON SAFEGUARDING PROPERTY

- Never pack valuables in your hold luggage: theft from the hold is not uncommon.
- Store your hand luggage in the overhead locker opposite your seat and not in the locker directly above your seat. This way you will be able to keep an eye on your bag and anyone who might be tempted to interfere with it.
- Always try to keep valuables such as your phone and money on your person. If you do have to store them in your hand luggage, make sure you check that they are still there before the aircraft lands and passengers disembark. There are people who make a living from robbing other passengers while the aircraft is in flight. They know that people often carry large sums of money and valuables in their hand luggage, so will wait until passengers are asleep before having a rummage through their bags.
- If you do find that something has been stolen, immediately alert a member of the cabin crew before people are able to leave the aircraft, and encourage other passengers to check their bags too. The chances are that, if you have been robbed, so have others, and there's strength in numbers when it comes to getting the cabin crew to do something about it.

CHAPTER THREE

KIDNAP AWARENESS AND AVOIDANCE

Kidnapping is a profitable business. Some public policy groups estimate that around the world each year more than 100,000 kidnappings take place, worth over £325 million (US$500 million) in ransoms. Figures regarding the scale of it are often inaccurate, though, since for a variety of reasons many crimes of this nature go unreported by both governments and victims.

What makes it even harder to get a handle on the situation is the fact that there are different forms of kidnapping, and most are a million miles from the type we tend to see in the movies, where someone has a hood shoved over their head and is then bundled into the boot (trunk) of a car. There are much simpler techniques that involve lower risk to the kidnappers than forcing someone into a vehicle in a public place.

There are parts of Asia and Latin America where 'virtual kidnappings' are rife. Here, criminal gangs simply *claim* to have abducted someone and demand a ransom. If these incidents come to the notice of the police at all, they may end up on the charge sheet as fraud, rather than kidnapping. Elsewhere, there is what has become known as 'express kidnapping'. This often happens when the victim gets into a taxi: he or she is joined by a couple of heavies known to the driver, driven to an ATM and forced to withdraw the maximum daily amount from the machine. They are often held in very poor conditions (it's not unheard of for them to be kept in the boot of the car) until their bank accounts have been emptied. If they are lucky they are released, by which time they have been robbed of all their possessions, including their passport. In some regions this gets logged by the authorities as robbery rather than kidnap.

Whatever form they take, abductions of travellers are undoubtedly on the rise. It's an issue tourists can't ignore but it's especially serious for business travellers, who are frequently prime targets. A range of factors is fuelling the trend, such as serious economic and social inequality, terrorism and criminality. The poor, desperate and criminally minded have identified travellers as a good source of easy money and in some areas have turned kidnap into a thriving business. The rewards for kidnappers can be significant and the risk minimal.

Popular tourist spots in many countries are prime hunting grounds for kidnappers; not least because they are often located in poorer regions, populated by organised criminals, rebel groups or plain thugs. They also provide a regular source of income in the form of the tourists who travel to these places.

Once again, this chapter is not advocating that you should avoid high-risk areas altogether: the point is to help you make adequate advance preparations and, if the worst happens, give you strategies to deal with it.

MY STORY

The war in Colombia in the late 1990s made it a dangerous place. The situation for travellers wasn't helped by the US intervention, which was aimed at fighting drug cartels in their own backyard. Non-Latinos were viewed with suspicion or seen as fair targets for criminals and kidnappers. Either way, this wasn't a place you could afford to be lax about your personal security.

I met my friend Maverick at a hotel in Cartagena and told him I had filed our travel plans with the British Embassy and the expedition company in the UK we were carrying out the recce for. The FCO had recently relaxed its advice for the region we were in and as is normal in the adventure travel market, expedition providers want to be the first to offer new and exciting destinations to their customers. However, before they can do so, they need people like Mav and me to go and check it out first. I had also informed them as to when we intended to be back from our travels. If we didn't check in at the appropriate time, they would at least know we were missing and what our route had been. This came in particularly handy just a few days into the trip when the regions of Armenia and Pereira were hit by a massive earthquake that caused catastrophic damage, killing 1,000 people, injuring over 4,000 and leaving 200,000 homeless. The quake was global news, so it was only natural that friends and family put two and two together and were concerned over our safety.

My dad, being an ex-military man, knew what to do and called the British Embassy in Bogotá. They were able to confirm that our travel plans would not have taken us near the regions affected by the disaster. For our part, we had no idea that there had even been a quake until we arrived back in Cartagena weeks after the event.

Our journey had taken us to the far north of the country, to the coastal town of Santa Marta at the foot of the Sierra Nevada de Santa Marta mountains. Santa Marta was the starting point for expeditions to Ciudad Perdida (the Lost City), which was originally founded in about 800AD but abandoned when the Spanish Conquistadors arrived. It remained hidden until 1972, when it was 'rediscovered'. Getting there is not easy: it involves a six-day trek through the jungle and up into the mountains.

The trekking and terrain were not the major problem: the greatest danger came from the conflict between the government and the rebels. Colombia's internal conflict was being played out in the Sierra Nevada, and the various guerrilla groups were pursuing a deadly game of cat and mouse with the Colombian National Army (CNA).

We spent a lot of time trying to find out whether or not it would be safe to embark on the trek and we employed a local mountain guide to give us some credible information. Juan had been leading expeditions in the region for nearly ten years and knew the local people in the Sierra Nevada well. He also knew that getting his clients kidnapped or killed was bad for business, so he took their safety very seriously.

Juan told us that the route to the Lost City was currently in the hands of the Revolutionary Armed Forces of Colombia (FARC) and that the CNA was keen to change that. Although he was hoping to get us to the area, he was more intent on keeping us in one piece. Each evening he would come to the hotel where we were staying and give us a security update on whether or not it was safe to attempt the journey to the Lost City.

On our first night in town, Juan also provided us with information about safety in Santa Marta itself. He told us that after dark it was OK to turn left out of the hotel, but turn right and we would most likely end up dead. He warned us that there was a lot of trouble in Santa Marta at that time, with many vendetta killings taking place. It seemed that the Colombian method of dealing with enemies was to have them assassinated. This would then prompt the family of the victim to issue a vendetta against the person who had ordered the original killing and have them bumped off. This would go on back and forth until a truce was finally agreed between the rival factions.

When I asked who carried out the killings, Juan's response startled me.

'Usually the police,' he said nonchalantly.

'You're joking,' I said, genuinely shocked. 'I used to be a police officer.'

Juan did his best to explain.

'The police here are very poorly paid,' he said, 'and sometimes don't get paid at all, so they have to subsidise their living. Some police officers will carry out the killings for both parties, which is good business for them and means the investigation never finds the killer.'

Juan spoke so matter-of-factly that I had no reason to disbelieve him.

That evening when I went to bed, I wondered whether it was worth even trying to get to the Lost City. Over the next few hours, we were woken several times by gunfire: Santa Marta was clearly having a bad night.

Juan came to the hotel the next morning while we were having breakfast and told us that a number of taxi drivers had been murdered in robberies recently, and that their surviving colleagues had driven en masse to the city limits to hold a rally to highlight the issue. En route to the rally, two more taxi drivers had been murdered, so they had all headed back into Santa Marta in an attempt to find those responsible. Then the shooting really started. In the space of just one week, 23 people had been murdered in Santa Marta. That was pretty normal by Santa Marta standards according to Juan.

Juan also had bad news about our trek: there was fighting in the Lost City area, so any hopes of making it there were now dashed. Instead, he had sorted out an itinerary for us to travel to another part of the Sierra Nevada, trekking through pristine forest and staying in local communities for a week.

I asked about potential risk factors and Juan assured me that there were no troops or rebels in the area. He had arranged guides for us, and a donkey to carry all our equipment.

After satisfying ourselves that it was safe to do so, we set off with Juan from Santa Marta to a village on the edge of the jungle where we met our guide, Lionel, and his grey donkey. We spent time going over our route with Lionel and some of the other villagers before saying farewell to Juan and informing the British Embassy and expedition company of our route and schedule. We arranged a rendezvous point for the end of the week and then headed out into the jungle with Lionel and the donkey.

The scenery was stunning and I was amazed by the prolific birdlife. Toucans and macaws seemed to be everywhere and it was hard to imagine how such a beautiful country could be at war with itself.

The next few days saw us trekking further into the mountains and further away from civilisation. There was a feeling of splendid isolation, and there is always something magical about crossing rivers and hacking your way through jungle.

Towards the end of the fifth day we arrived at a small community, which was simply a collection of huts with chickens running around them. Lionel told us that we would sleep here, so out came the hammocks and Maverick and I headed to the nearby stream to have a wash. The water in the stream was cold but very refreshing, so we stayed there a while enjoying the last rays of the fading sun. By the time we got back to the huts, I could see that some other travellers had joined us. The difference was that these travellers were dressed in combat clothing and had assault rifles. Shit!

They eyed us with real suspicion as we headed towards them. I knew it would be no good to run or hide, so we walked confidently forwards, or as confidently as we could when dressed only in surf shorts and flip-flops. I couldn't help but hope that, if they did decide to kidnap us, they would at least let us change first. I was totally inappropriately dressed for life as a hostage.

I greeted them with a friendly '*Hola*'.

'*De donde eres?*' [Where are you from?] was the terse response.

No time for pleasantries then.

I explained that we were from the UK and were trekking

in the region as part of a holiday. They didn't believe us and accused us of being American.

'CIA? DEA?' they barked.

Bollocks! If they thought we were anything to do with the US government we were as good as dead. The expressions on their faces told me that they were serious.

'*No, no, soy de Inglaterra*,' I insisted.

Fortunately, Maverick's Spanish was better than mine and he spoke to them calmly about where we were from and why we were in Colombia. He also told them that we had British passports and so could prove to them that we weren't American.

I walked towards my bag, gesturing that I was going to get something out, and waited for their approval. The last thing I wanted was for them to think I was reaching for a weapon. One of them nodded that it was OK and I pulled out my passport. He snatched it from me and opened it, checking my photo against my face before passing it round to the other gunmen to have a look.

'*Inglaterra*, eh?' one of them asked.

'*Si, Inglaterra*,' I responded.

Mav then got his passport out and they passed that around the group. They suddenly became very interested in Mav's passport. They looked at one another. Mav and I also looked at one another. Was something wrong?

'Manchester?' one questioned quite excitedly.

Mav had been born in Manchester.

'*Si*, Manchester,' replied Mav.

'Manchester United?' another quizzed Maverick further.

'*Si, si*, Manchester United!' explained Mav with a smile.

Then the man I suspected of being the leader said, 'David Beckham?'

'*Si, si*,' I replied. 'David Beckham.'

We started talking to them about David Beckham and as Mav was from Manchester, they were impressed that they were in the presence of someone who had actually been to Old Trafford.

The mood lightened somewhat after that but they still kept our passports, which made me nervous. Lionel tried to calm the situation by producing a bottle of poor-quality local rum and gesturing for everyone to take a seat. One by one we sat down and Lionel started a fire and poured the rum. At first the conversation was stilted and I wasn't at all sure how this was going to turn out. There's only so much you can say about David Beckham and Manchester United. However, as the night went on, the atmosphere became more relaxed, and by the time Lionel produced a second bottle of terrible rum, there was a lot of laughter.

The additional guests turned out to be part of a local militia who protected communities within the area from the CNA troops and various rebel groups. They knew that they didn't stand a chance in a fire fight against any of these, but they did provide a deterrent. They told us stories of how some of their brothers had joined the FARC while others had been conscripted into the army, so that members of the same family were fighting on opposite sides. It was no wonder the country had so many issues. They wanted to know about Britain, about the Queen and, of course, about David Beckham.

It was an interesting evening and after a few hours they handed us back our passports and bade us farewell. Then, as suddenly as they had appeared, they drifted back into the jungle. Once they were gone, Lionel told us that they had been following us for most of the day. It was eerie to think that we had been stalked without knowing anything about it.

A few days later, our journey with Lionel and his donkey came to an end. Waiting for us at the edge of the jungle was Juan, just as we had agreed. He had arranged for us to spend a few days in the Tayrona National Park, staying in a hut on the beach. After a week in the jungle sleeping in flea-ridden hammocks, it was just what we needed and I looked forward to the change.

Tayrona is an area of outstanding beauty and the scenery was breathtaking, with the contrast between the richness of the forest and the crystal clear waters of the Caribbean Sea. We spent our first few days taking walks along the beach and in the forest. The people were amazingly friendly and it was hard to believe that this was the same country that had so many problems.

On our penultimate day, we were spending the early evening at a picnic table having a few beers with a couple of people we had met. I sat with my back to the ocean, looking up at the forest. The sun was setting but the air was still warm; the company and conversation were good and the beers were slipping down very nicely. It was a perfect evening.

We had started to construct a pyramid with the empty beer cans and our creation was nearing completion when suddenly everything changed. People started running about in blind panic and then came the unmistakable sound of gunshots piercing the evening air.

The four of us remained at our table and at first struggled to see what was going on. Then, not more than 20 yards (18m) directly in front of me, I saw two people being dragged out from behind the bar by a group of men armed with handguns, and made to kneel on the ground. Two of our group, including Maverick, had their backs to the bar. Maverick asked me what was happening. I told them both not to turn around as it would draw attention to us and described the scene to them in a whisper.

The two men were still on their knees and seemed to be pleading with the gunmen. For their part, the gunmen were shouting at their captives and were clearly not happy about something. The men kept pleading and held their hands up to their chests as if in prayer.

A shot rang out.

'What happened?' asked Mav.

Before I could answer there came another shot.

'They've just slotted them,' I responded.

One of the captors had walked up behind each of the men in turn, put a gun to his head and pulled the trigger. His actions looked almost mechanical. The place was silent for a while and I stared ahead, barely believing what I had seen: two men summarily executed just 20 yards away from me.

The silence was broken by more shouting as a third man was dragged out. He was taken into the forest by the gunmen. As soon as they had gone, I ran to my hut and grabbed the medical kit that I always carry. I knew there was little chance that anyone had survived and in hindsight it seemed like a pretty futile gesture, but my instinct was to see what I could do to help.

When I reached the two bodies it was obvious that their injuries were incompatible with life. The bullets had removed part of their skulls and their brains were on the ground. A few people were screaming and crying, and there was nothing I could do.

We heard more screaming from the forest as the third man pleaded for his life and then the sound of another shot, followed by a chilling silence.

I started to move in the direction of the sound but was stopped by a Colombian woman who worked in the park.

'Don't go in there,' she warned. 'There's nothing you can do and they might hurt you too. This is a Colombian problem, not yours.'

She was right. There was nothing we could do.

Mav turned to me, putting one of his huge arms around my shoulders, and said, 'Come on, mate, there's nothing we can do for these poor bastards. Let's go back and have a beer. I think we could both do with one.'

So that's what we did. We went to the bar, which had now reopened, bought a few beers and finished off our pyramid. The whole event seemed totally surreal.

We left Tayrona the next day with the images of the previous night still fresh in our minds. They had found the body of the third man in the forest, with a single bullet wound to the head. The killers had been consistent if nothing else. By the time we got back to Santa Marta all I wanted to do was have a shower and another beer.

The next morning Juan met us in the hotel. He had the local paper with him. On the front page were photos of the three dead men on slabs in the morgue with the headline: 'Death comes to Paradise'.

The dead men had apparently been robbing tourists and therefore badly affecting visitor numbers. A group of men who made an honest living from working in the park had got together a few months previously and told these men to leave. The robbers had initially heeded the warning, knowing that the consequences of staying would be harsh. However, their greed brought them back and they started robbing tourists again, giving a bad name to Tayrona and affecting the livelihoods of those who lived and worked there. On our last night in the park, the Colombian version of justice caught up with them and they were 'dispatched'. It was a harsh lesson for us that travelling to such places can be fraught with risk.

We stayed in Colombia for a few more weeks and, despite what happened in Tayrona, I still maintain it is one of the most beautiful places I have ever been to, and with some of the friendliest people I have ever met. Since our time there, Colombia has become a much safer place to visit and I am pleased to say that travellers from all over the world are now starting to enjoy its treasures.

IMPROVING THE ODDS

There are lessons to be learnt when travelling to places where crime is rife and life is cheap. Things could have turned out very differently for us in Colombia.

In 2003, for example, a group of tourists trekking to the Lost City were kidnapped and held for over 100 days in the very same jungle which, on Juan's advice, Maverick and I had decided to avoid. The kidnappers were Colombia's second largest rebel group, the National Liberation Army, and the tourists were forced to walk through the jungle for up to 18 hours a day to avoid coming into contact with government forces. They were only released after intensive international negotiations. Theirs was a tough ordeal in very uncomfortable conditions, with little food apart from rice. Even now, more than ten years since their release, a number of them still suffer psychologically.

The first thing you need to determine when you are planning a trip is whether or not you are likely to be a target. The bad news is that, whenever you travel to a developing country, the answer is probably a resounding 'yes'. It is very dangerous to assume that, just because you don't think you are very wealthy, you won't attract potential kidnappers. You may not feel wealthy by your home country's standards but in a poorer country you may seem very well off indeed.

I'd urge everyone to do some pre-travel due diligence. Use the internet to look up your destination, check travel warnings and look into signs of potential trouble.

Before you arrive at your intended destination get a good and trusted local contact, or fixer, in place. If you are travelling on business, other companies or security specialists who have worked in the region should be able to recommend someone reliable. In Colombia, Juan was great and came with a strong recommendation from others who had worked in the area previously.

However, a word of warning about fixers: not all local contacts can be relied upon and there have been a number of cases where the local contact has been responsible for setting up for kidnap the people they were supposedly working for. Again, you can do a lot to protect yourself if you do research on your destination and the people you will be working with, and take precautions to avoid becoming a target. If you feel you are a high-risk target or are travelling to a high-risk region, you would be wise to take a kidnap awareness and avoidance course before you go.

The time you are at your most vulnerable is when you first arrive in a new country. Never get into a vehicle with someone you don't know or haven't got a means of identifying. It's always best to arrange in advance to be met by a driver, and to make sure you have a way of confirming that the person who meets you is, indeed, the driver. It's not unknown for kidnappers to copy the names of arriving passengers from the signs which genuine drivers hold up in arrivals halls, and then to manoeuvre their way into a position to meet the passenger before the real driver does. I always use a password system when I am being met, and will often arrange with the transport company that we meet at a café in the airport, thus avoiding the mayhem that is usually prevalent in arrivals halls. This makes it much easier for me to assess whether the driver is, in fact, bona fide. Don't forget that inside the terminal building there's a degree of security. It's once you get outside that it really can become a free-for-all.

It's also worth using technology to your advantage. Tell your driver that it's policy for you to take a photo of him and his vehicle (particularly the number plate) and email them to someone at home before you get into the vehicle. That way, if he is part of a potential kidnap plot, he'll have second thoughts. Just make sure that you tell the person you send the email to your intended journey time – and also let them know when you've arrived safely at your destination.

Thereafter, as you begin to feel more at home in the country, don't let your growing familiarity with the area lull you into dropping your guard. Keep a low profile, don't advertise your wealth or status, dress down and blend in. Mix up your times and routines by travelling along different roads, eating at different restaurants, trying out different bars and cafés at varying times. Be especially wary in isolated and rural areas, and remain vigilant at all times. Do not become time and route predictable. Kidnappers will often carry out surveillance on their intended targets for extended periods before taking them. Be suspicious of anyone you feel is following you or monitoring your movements.

WHAT TO DO IF IT ALL GOES WRONG

Kidnapping is a terrifying experience. Not only is it psychologically traumatic for the victim but, especially during the early phase of the event, the kidnappers will be exceptionally edgy. Don't risk antagonising them.

If you are taken, the best defence is passive cooperation, and it's vital that you humanise yourself to your kidnappers. During the incident in Colombia, I was very conscious of the need to find common ground with the militia as soon as possible. You need to get them to see (and treat) you as a human being and not a piece of merchandise. Research has clearly demonstrated that kidnappers are less inclined to harm those with whom they have something in common, so try to establish some sort of rapport. Football, especially David Beckham, worked well for me but family is a universal subject. I would steer clear of politics and religion, but if they do raise those subjects, listen attentively to their point of view.

Plan from the beginning for the possibility that your ordeal may be lengthy, and work out how you can keep track of the passage of time. You may be handled roughly and this could involve being hooded or blindfolded and being segregated from others who may have been taken with you. Your captors may try to confuse you by taking your watch, keeping you in a windowless room or serving meals at odd times. You can get an approximate idea of passing time from, say, the temperature changes between night and day or by listening to outside noises such as traffic or birdsong. It's vital to remember that at some point you are likely to have to give up physical control, therefore it's imperative that you retain psychological control.

Whilst you're in captivity focus your mind on the positive aspects of your daily life, even if these are few and far between. Give yourself a project to occupy your mind. During nearly five years as a hostage, Terry Waite spent time 'writing' a book in his head, meditating and maintaining a daily exercise routine.

Look after your physical health too. Eat the food provided without complaint, exercise if you can and ask for medical treatment or medicines if you need them.

Take careful note of the characteristics of your kidnappers, such as their habits, speech and contacts, as well as of your surroundings. This information could prove invaluable later on in assisting the authorities to prevent future incidents.

KIDNAP SAFETY CHECKLIST

- Ensure that you always inform a trusted source of your travel plans, especially if these plans are subject to change. This could be your office, a friend or a family member. That way, if they don't hear from you or can't get hold of you, they can quickly raise the alarm.
- Learn to lower your profile and blend in with your surroundings. Try not to look too much like a tourist or business traveller. Learn to be 'grey'.
- Look out for signs of surveillance. If you think you are being watched, you probably are.
- Closely guard your personal information and be careful with whom you share it. Certainly don't give out your address, details of family members or your job title. All these will help inform potential kidnappers of your net worth. Even your business

card contains key information about who you are and what you might be worth.

- When you leave clubs and bars at night, especially if you are the worse for wear, you will be an easy and vulnerable target. Don't leave alone and make sure you have transport and a safe route home.

- If you are in one place for a while, make sure that you vary your routine and daily schedule. Don't always leave your accommodation at the same time every day and don't take the same route to and from work, the gym, the coffee shop and so on. Make it difficult for any potential kidnapper to chart your movements. Be unpredictable.

- There are some great tracking devices on the market these days and many of them are quite discreet. Some of them combine a GPS unit (which you might have as part of your kit anyway) with an SOS device, which you can activate in case of trouble. However, bear in mind that if you are taken you will be searched and any such devices will be discovered and sent in the opposite direction to where you are going to be held.

- Some kidnaps are opportunistic, so the key to kidnap avoidance is to deprive potential kidnappers as far as possible of opportunity. Don't use ATMs on the street: instead go into a bank. And, where possible, move around with other people. There's strength in numbers and being in a group will certainly make you a less attractive target.

- A privately owned car offers the best security but avoid luxury or ostentatious vehicles. Blend in by using the type of car favoured by locals. Keep the vehicle in good repair and the petrol tank at least half full.

- If you are taken, try to connect with your captors, where possible, by using their first names and encouraging them to use yours. Find a common bond with them and make it easy for them to like you. It's a good tactic for minimising the de-humanising effect. Psychologically, it's harder for them to harm someone they know personally. Avoid disagreement with them, or antagonising them.

- Although you will not be able to see evidence of it, the strong likelihood is that negotiations will be underway for your release. However, hostage negotiation is a long and complicated process, so do all you can to remain positive that others are doing all they can to help you.
- Don't forget to negotiate for small items of comfort, as these will be big psychological wins for you during your captivity if you manage to get them.

CHAPTER FOUR

PERSONAL SAFETY AND SECURITY

Much as we like to think that our journeys begin with a flight, sea passage or overland trip, they actually start long before that, or at least they should do. Planning for travel should form a major part of your safety and security procedures. All too often people embark on a trip without knowing enough about the potential dangers that await them at their destination, and these can range from the pickpocket at the local station to natural disasters. Both have the potential to ruin your day – or worse.

While most travellers nowadays research visas and vaccinations as a matter of course before their departure, I also like to familiarise myself in advance with my future surroundings. I'd certainly want to make sure when I arrive at a destination that I have a good stock of maps before I venture out to explore (and if you don't fancy carrying around heavy maps, there are plenty of web-based apps available).

However, nothing says 'I'm new here and don't know where I'm going' more than a tourist holding a map, and this identifies you as a potential target. I always familiarise myself with the local street map *before* going on a recce of a new town or city. If you have a good look at the map ahead of time, it will also help you plan a rough itinerary. You don't have to stick to it religiously but it will stop you wandering aimlessly.

Consider learning at least a few phrases in the local tongue if English isn't the native language of your destination. It will help you to blend in better, plus it's a great way to immerse yourself in your new environment. Locals will really appreciate the effort too. Similarly, research the local culture so you know what is expected of you with regards to clothing, body language and attitude. It's also worth keeping a close eye on world events via news channels, government advice and social media, in case there's a possibility of local unrest that could make the environment dangerously unstable.

Of course, no one wants to expect the worst and sometimes things will happen which you won't be able to prevent. By thinking ahead, however, you can reduce the chances of untoward incidents and be ready to act appropriately should something go wrong.

Always invest in adequate insurance cover for your trip. This should include all activities you intend to undertake during the period as well as adequate cover for medical treatment and, in a worst-case scenario, repatriation.

MY STORY

After my trip to Colombia, it wasn't long before I had cause to concentrate again on my personal security. My next trip would be from my base in Lima to Patagonian Chile and Argentina. Once again, I was researching new expedition routes and the plan was to fly into Santiago in Chile and then down to Punta Arenas, where I would hire a car. This would allow me the flexibility and freedom to cover the huge area of Patagonia in both Chile and Argentina. I was delighted that I was going to have the best part of a month for the trip, because there are few more spectacular places on the planet to explore than Patagonia. However, as ever, I was very aware that the more thoroughly I planned and researched in advance, the better would be my chances of avoiding unpleasant situations.

Although I had planned meticulously and was keeping a close eye on the political situation in Chile, my arrival happened to coincide with the day its former president, General Pinochet, was arrested in London for human rights violations. The streets of Santiago were suddenly full of pro-Pinochet supporters who were enraged by Britain (which they had once seen as an ally) having the gall to arrest their former leader. Riots had broken out all over the city.

I was blissfully unaware that anything was wrong when I arrived at the airport, and the first I knew of it was when the taxi I took to my hotel dumped me and my bags in the middle of a very hostile crowd in downtown Santiago.

The driver gave me a final word of advice before driving off.

'Your hotel is over there.' He pointed to some buildings on the other side of the rioters and then added, somewhat unhelpfully, 'Just don't tell anyone you are British.'

With that he sped away.

Almost immediately, I was confronted by an angry mob, many of whom were burning British flags and chanting anti-British slogans. I was aware that, in the distance, the police were doing their best to break up the riot with water cannon and tear gas, but I couldn't see how they would be in a position to help me any time soon.

In order to get to my hotel, I had to weave my way through the mob. I set my shoulders in the right direction and began to walk through the crowd with grim determination.

I was nearly at the hotel entrance when a group of particularly thuggish looking protesters blocked my path. Just a few moments before they had been focused on making petrol bombs – but now they seemed very interested in me. Despite the potential severity of the circumstances, I couldn't help reflecting how they reminded me of 1980s-era British skinheads.

'Where are you from?' demanded one of the larger protesters, speaking in English.

I stood frozen for a moment, thinking back to what the taxi driver had told me. Then I looked him straight in the eye and, putting on my best approximation of an Irish accent, said, 'I'm from Ireland, mate. We've been fighting the Brits for years.'

The protesters patted me on the back as a sign of solidarity and let me on my way.

I spent the remainder of the day watching the riot from my hotel room. There must have been a TV camera crew on the roof of the hotel, as the coverage beamed to my TV matched what I was seeing outside my window.

By a very odd coincidence, the next time I travelled to Santiago was the day the British House of Lords announced that Pinochet would not be held responsible for crimes committed after 1988, which effectively meant most of those for which he had been indicted. As a result, this time the anti-Pinochet brigade were out on the streets, rioting against Britain's decision.

I knew the drill now and once again made my way safely through the mob to my hotel and watched the riot from there. However, I made a conscious note to check the news more carefully before travelling to any foreign country, especially Chile.

IMPROVING THE ODDS

Large demonstrations – and, to state the obvious, riots – should be avoided at all costs. Trouble can ignite very quickly, and once you are caught up in a mob, it can be very difficult to extricate yourself. Crowd situations seem to take on a life of their own and you can very quickly and easily get sucked into the flow of events and dragged along against your will. It's like trying to swim against a riptide.

Demonstrations and public-order situations are not, of course, the only potential safety hazards you should consider. All travellers need to adopt at all times what the security industry refers to as 'situational awareness', which is defined as: 'being aware of what is happening around you in terms of where you are, where you are supposed to be, and whether anyone or anything around you is a threat to your safety and security.... This means that everyone's situational awareness is individual and potentially different.'

More simply put, this means knowing what's going on around you and who or what are threats to you. It's impossible to operate at a heightened level of vigilance all the time, but you should get into the habit of continually assessing potential threats and having a plan as to how you might deal with them.

When you are caught up in the excitement of exploring new places, it is very easy to relax and forget all about maintaining a situational awareness of the environment you're in. Many travellers, wherever they are in the world, automatically default to the way they would behave at home. These people are easy-pickings for criminals and those who seek to exploit travellers. By being off guard they leave themselves completely vulnerable.

When we arrive in a new location, particularly one we've never visited before, we have little to no idea of what is normal. It takes us a little time to familiarise ourselves with our new surroundings, and this is the time when we are most vulnerable. We need to align ourselves with a baseline of what is normal; only then can we spot the danger signals of what is out of the ordinary. Anybody who travels to Rome for the first time would think the standard of driving is insane, but after a few days it is very normal... for Rome.

In our hometowns we understand and know what is normal without even thinking about it, which allows us to spot very quickly when something isn't right, or out of place. This allows us to take evasive action if we think that we are in danger. However, when we arrive somewhere new, we don't have the advantage of this inbuilt early warning system, so we have to develop it and this takes time.

Remember: criminals almost always carry out in advance their assessments as to who they are going to target. Crime is very rarely a random act. Criminals always opt for the easy goal rather than risk acting against someone who is going to present more of a challenge. Like animals selecting prey, the less desirable elements of society look to target the weak and defenceless. Therefore the more you can do to reduce your appeal, the less likely you are to be targeted.

I plan every step of every journey and know exactly where I need to be and when. If something happens to delay me, I have contingencies in place. I always make sure that I look as though I know what I'm doing and where I'm going, even if I'm visiting a place for the first time. If you look calm and confident, you are less likely to attract criminals. They will focus on the lost and vulnerable.

It's not all down to planning, though. I would urge any traveller to always listen to their gut instinct. If a situation doesn't feel right to you, there's probably a reason for that, so do something about it. Human beings have an innate ability to recognise danger. However, as we have become more civilised, we have lost the capacity to act upon the primal instinct of fear. Trust your intuition and, more importantly, act on it. Far too often have I heard victims of crime say things like, 'I knew there was something dodgy about him' or 'There was something not quite right' after an incident has occurred. That's their gut instinct talking, but they have chosen to override it and then got themselves into trouble.

Obviously you can't go through life mistrusting everyone you come into contact with and part of the joy of travel is meeting local people and trusting them. I have taken many journeys with local people I hardly know and stayed in many communities where I just had to trust they would look after me. In the vast majority of cases these interactions have been trouble-free and highly enjoyable. But have a plan in mind for uncomfortable situations, and make sure you always have an exit strategy in case you need to employ it.

WHAT TO DO IF IT ALL GOES WRONG

If things do go wrong, it is important to remain calm. Most problems are easy to deal with, particularly if you've done your preparation. If you lose your passport or it's stolen, contact your nearest embassy or consulate about getting a replacement. If your credit cards disappear, get in touch with your bank so that they can be cancelled. Be sure to keep your bank's emergency number with you and not just on your phone contacts list: otherwise, if your phone is stolen at the same time, you'll be in real trouble.

If you do become a victim of crime, report it to the local police and get a written acknowledgement from them as well as a reference number. You will need this in order to make an insurance claim.

In the unlikely event that civil unrest should break out while you are visiting a country, make your way to your accommodation as quickly as you can or, if you are already there, remain where you are. Use the internet to check in with the Foreign & Commonwealth Office travel advice pages to get their assessment of the situation and, if in doubt, contact your embassy in-country to ask for its advice. Don't be tempted to wander around outside to check out what's going on.

PERSONAL SAFETY AND SECURITY CHECKLIST

- Always tell someone where you're going, what your intended route is and how long your journey is likely to be. (This can be your embassy or consulate, or a friend or family member.) Arrange regular call-in times with a trusted person to let them know you are safe – and stick to them.
- Never display signs of wealth. Things like cameras slung over shoulders or expensive watches on wrists identify you as a potential target. Keep money, wallets, purses and money belts

under clothing and not in pockets. Some people make a living from pickpocketing.

- Consider carrying a 'false' or 'dummy' wallet that you can hand over if you are robbed. This should contain an expired credit/ debit card and a small amount of cash in low-denomination notes. Robbers rarely check the contents thoroughly at the scene of the crime.
- Keep your bags with you at all times and don't trust them to strangers to guard, even if this means you have to take them into the toilet with you.
- Keep all medications in your hand luggage. It's also worth bringing along a copy of your prescription and a letter from your doctor in case you lose your medication.
- Identify safe havens or points of safety in the local vicinity. These are places that you can head to if you get into trouble or need help or to get out of harm's way, such as a hotel, police station, hospital, embassy or place of worship.
- Listen to local advice. Locals will have the most up-to-date information as to which places are safe and where danger lurks. Be aware, though, that not all natives are necessarily friendly and some may pretend to befriend you for nefarious reasons. Other travellers are also a great source of information, particularly if they have just come from a place to which you are heading.
- Avoid demonstrations and civil disturbances at all costs.
- Never get involved in handling or using illegal drugs. You will most likely end up in a foreign prison.
- Familiarise yourself with local laws as they may be very different from the laws you are used to. Remember that it is the law of the land you're in that applies, not the law you may be familiar with at home.

A FEW WORDS ABOUT SOCIAL MEDIA

I often hold my head in my hands when the holiday season is in full swing: so many people can't seem to resist the temptation of sharing their holiday photos with their friends and family on social media. What better way could there be to show off your beach body than with pictures of you lapping up the sun, sea and sand while those left at home continue with the nine-to-five drudgery? Or so the thinking goes.

Of course, another way of looking at it is that it's a great way of letting people who may not be such good friends know that you are away from home and that your house is empty.

Criminals have long used social media as a tool to ascertain when people are away and therefore which properties are worth targeting. And if your car is left on your driveway, that raises the chances of it being 'stolen to order'.

You wouldn't stick a big sign outside your house saying, 'Away on holiday for the next two weeks' – so why post something on your Facebook page that conveys the same message?

Don't be lulled into a false sense of security of thinking that it's only your friends and connections who can see your posts. In many cases this is simply not true. Depending on your security settings, you should also be asking yourself who can see what your friends are 'liking' and 'sharing' with others. It's entirely possible that you won't even know the people who end up reading your fabulous holiday diary and who, more to the point, know where you live.

A recent survey carried out in the United States showed that 75 per cent of convicted burglars admitted to using social media as a tool to identify properties to target. If you are posting live details of where you are and what you are doing, you are doing half their work for them.

Most burglaries are opportunistic and burglars like to be in and out of a property within ten minutes. However, if they know that they're unlikely to be disturbed, they will take their time in making sure they find all the higher value items.

It's not just criminals who are wising up to the use of social media in the commission of crimes. Insurance companies are also tightening up their terms and conditions. There have been a number of cases recently where insurance companies have declined claims following a burglary because they have been able to demonstrate that the victim posted on social media the fact that they were away.

All of the above also applies when you are travelling on business, perhaps doubly so. I regularly see posts from people saying they are kicking back in the business-class lounge of such and such an international airport, about to head off to a far-flung destination. Not only does that inform criminals at home that these people are away but it also provides criminals at their destination with the very useful tip-off that a (probably well-off) business-class traveller flying on a particular airline is heading their way. In such a case you might well be targeted long before you land.

SO WHAT'S THE SOLUTION?

As a rule, never post your address online, not even the street name. It's easy enough as it is to do a search on a person's name and find out where they live, so don't make it even easier for criminals. I would also turn off the location-sharing features on all your electronic devices. Why would you want to give people information about just how far away you are from your house and valuables?

When you are planning a trip, boost your home security by installing an alarm and buying a timer for your lights. Only tell those who really need to know when and where you are going. This might include a trusted friend or neighbour who can go and check on your property during your absence, collect your mail and open and close your curtains.

Next, don't post anything at all to social media while you are actually away. Take the time to enjoy your holiday and get a break from your electronic gadgets. There's no reason not to share your travel experiences and photos with friends on social media, but do it when you've returned from your holiday or business trip. Just be sure that you make it clear in the way you word your post that you are now back home ('Just got back from a great holiday in…').

Your friends will still be jealous of your tan, even if you've been back a week. And it's far better to delay your social media posts than to get home to find that your house has been burgled.

CHAPTER FIVE

NATURAL DISASTERS

Nature has a number of ways of putting us in our place and reminding us that we are not the most powerful species on the planet. These reminders occasionally take the most spectacular forms, such as hurricanes, earthquakes, volcanoes and tsunamis, and can cause a large number of casualties in a relatively short space of time, as well as tremendous damage to property and the environment. I refer to such events as 'geohazards' and they should certainly be taken into account in any pre-travel planning.

Thankfully, natural disasters are relatively rare and your chances of being involved in one are exceptionally low. When they do strike, however, they can do so with tremendous force and often without much warning. Therefore the more prepared you are, the greater your chances of survival.

Geohazards can be totally indiscriminate and strike with little or no notice, although some areas of the world are more prone to certain types of natural events than others. Earthquakes in particular often occur with little warning, and while the risk of exposure from the impact of tsunamis is greatly reduced by tsunami warning systems, not all areas are covered. There are countless websites that detail areas of volatility, so it's worth doing a bit of research once you know your precise travel plans in order to arm yourself with the best available facts. Some types of geohazard, such as hurricanes, are seasonal and can be more easily tracked and monitored. You may find it wise to avoid particular areas at certain times of year.

MY STORY

I was leading an expedition in Peru. We had travelled from Lima along the coast via Paracas, Ica and Nazca to the coastal community of Puerto Inca and then on to Arequipa. The journey to Arequipa had taken a while, thanks to a number of landslides blocking the road in various places. Highway maintenance vehicles were often unable to get through, so clearing a route was left to the other road users, who formed temporary chain gangs to get traffic flowing again. It was tough and time-consuming work, and frustrating to get involved with clearing one blockage only to be confronted with another a few miles further into the journey.

By the time we reached Arequipa, the group I was leading was tired and dirty and only interested in grabbing something to eat and taking a shower. Compared to the coast where we had come from, Arequipa was cold, so most people decided to have an early night.

Just before dawn I was woken by a sensation I had never experienced before: the whole room was shaking. I sat up to try and get out of bed, but couldn't. The moment I put my foot on the ground, I had to quickly withdraw it and return it back inside the bed covers. The whole floor was juddering and I just couldn't get a foothold. It was the strangest feeling. The bed wasn't much better. It was shaking so violently it could have been in a scene from the horror movie *The Exorcist*. Then, all at once, all the pictures fell off the wall and the bedside lamps crashed to the ground.

It's hard to describe exactly how it all felt. I suppose I could say it was like being in a box that a very big person was shaking relentlessly from side to side. The overwhelming feeling I had was of knowing that I was not in control of this situation and never could be. Mother Nature had unleashed an earthquake and I was right in the middle of it.

My primary concern was my own safety, followed by the safety of my group. I knew that the recommended practice in earthquakes was to get underneath something, so I grabbed a blanket and dived under the bed. It didn't feel that safe and I felt like a little boy hiding from the bogeyman.

Then the shaking stopped. I stayed put for a short while and then decided to try and make it to the door to go and check on the group.

Just as I got to my feet, the shaking started again and this time it was stronger than before. I shot back under the bed, but I had only been there a matter of seconds before the shaking stopped again. This time I waited longer before venturing out, and then slowly made my way to the door, very conscious that I might have to make a dash for the bed again.

When I opened the door, a scene of carnage greeted me. Anything that hadn't been secured was spread all over the floor. Plant pots, pictures, lamps: everything had come crashing down. All of the windows had smashed and there was glass all over the place.

I was on the ground floor but my group was on the first floor. I looked up and saw them coming out of their rooms to survey the damage. A quick head count showed that they were all there and all completely unharmed. I issued instructions to remain in their rooms under their beds until we were given the all-clear, and then I returned to my room and followed my own advice.

There were a few aftershocks but these were nothing compared to the original quake.

When the all-clear was given I ventured out into the streets, where I saw further destruction. Fortunately for Arequipa, many of the buildings are constructed of a local white volcanic rock called 'sillar', which according to legend is earthquake-proof. Certainly, on the evidence before me, this appeared to be the case. Any building made of sillar looked relatively undamaged, while anything constructed of bricks and mortar or lesser material was in ruins.

The hotel we were staying in was thankfully made of sillar. The residents of Arequipa had got used to earthquakes over the centuries, so many buildings were constructed out of this remarkable rock. The locals have a nice saying about their sillar: 'When the moon separated from the earth, it left Arequipa behind.'

The quake had registered 6.8 on the Richter scale and the epicentre was 50 miles (80km) from Arequipa. Over 300 homes were destroyed and dozens of people were injured, but thankfully there were few deaths.

One member of my expedition was rather quiet for a while after the quake. When I asked him whether he was all right, he looked at me pensively.

After a few moments, he said, 'I just keep going over it in my head. What if the building had collapsed?'

I did my best to reassure him: 'Well, it didn't. We all survived and we're all safe.'

He looked rather confused and then went on, 'It's not that I'm so worried about. The trouble is, I sleep naked, and I keep having visions of my naked body being dragged from the rubble and being broadcast all over CNN. Do you know how embarrassing that would be for me? I live in a small village and everyone would be talking about it. Maybe I should get myself a pair of pyjamas.'

I agreed nightwear might be a wise idea and then headed off to find a phone that worked in order to inform HQ in the UK that we were all safe. The news had been full of the earthquake, and they were relieved to hear that everyone was OK. They could now let the families of those on my team know that they had heard from us and that their loved ones were unharmed and were continuing with the expedition.

EARTHQUAKES: IMPROVING THE ODDS

According to the US Geological Survey, globally there are over 275 earthquakes a day that are strong enough to be perceived by humans. (There are thousands more that are so weak we just don't feel them.) It's worth knowing what to do if you are ever caught up in one and to have a plan of action in place.

Most earthquake-related injuries and deaths result from falling debris, flying glass and collapsing structures such as buildings and bridges. Earthquakes can also trigger landslides, avalanches, flash floods, fires and tsunamis.

Identify safe places in the area where you are staying. Look for a sturdy table, for example, next to an interior wall. Stay well away from windows that could shatter and cause injury and from tall furniture that could fall on you. Keep in mind that, in modern buildings, doorways are no stronger than any other part of the structure. Additionally, there is the potential danger of injury from swinging doors.

EARTHQUAKES: WHAT TO DO IF IT ALL GOES WRONG

Current advice from New Zealand (and they know a thing or two about earthquakes there) on how to best protect yourself is to *drop, cover and hold*. Drop to the floor, cover your head and neck with your arms, get under something like a strong table and hold on to it to stop it moving away from you. Stay indoors until the shaking stops and you are sure it is safe to go out.

You may not be in the relative safety of a hotel room when an earthquake strikes, but the 'drop, cover and hold' advice applies pretty much anywhere you find yourself. If you are in an elevator, for example, drop, cover and hold. When the shaking stops, try to get out at the nearest floor if you can do so safely.

Do the same if you are outdoors when the shaking starts, moving a few steps away from buildings, trees, streetlights and power lines to avoid falling debris. If you are at a beach or near a coast, drop, cover and hold, then after the shaking stops move to higher ground immediately, in case a tsunami follows the quake. If you are in a mountainous area or near unstable slopes or cliffs, be alert for the possibility of falling debris or landslides.

If you are driving, pull over to a clear location, stop and stay there with your seat belt fastened until the shaking stops. Then proceed with caution, avoiding bridges or ramps that might have been damaged.

In the aftermath of the quake, tune in to local radio stations, because emergency-management officials will broadcast the most appropriate advice for your area. There may well be aftershocks.

Check yourself for injuries and get first aid if necessary. Help others if you can. Be aware that electricity supplies could be cut, and that fire alarms and sprinkler systems can go off in buildings during an earthquake even if there is no fire. Check for small fires and extinguish them.

If the building is damaged, make your way outside and find a safe open place. Use the stairs not the elevators. Keep eyes and ears open for potential hazards. There may be fallen power lines or broken gas lines, and you should stay well clear of damaged areas.

If you are still indoors and smell gas or hear a blowing or hissing noise, open a window, get everyone out quickly and turn off the gas if you can. If you see sparks, broken wires or evidence of damage to an electrical system, turn off the electricity at the main fuse box if it is safe to do so.

Only use landline and mobile phones for short essential calls so that lines are kept clear for emergency communications.

HURRICANES: IMPROVING THE ODDS

Hurricanes, typhoons, cyclones and tornadoes are all words used to describe the abnormally fast or turbulent wind systems that occur around the world. All should be avoided if at all possible. Not only do they bring high winds but they are also often accompanied by heavy rain and sea surges that increase the risk of flooding. When Hurricane Harvey made landfall in Texas in August 2017 it unleashed over 40 inches (1,000mm) of rain, causing massive flooding, which led to over 30,000 people being displaced. Just days later Hurricane Irma unleashed winds of over 180mph (290kph) as it slammed into the Caribbean, followed quickly by Hurricane Jose, which just compounded the misery for those caught up in the hurricanes before.

Early warning systems for such storms are now very advanced, and satellite images usually provide plenty of notice that a severe weather system is approaching. This should be your cue to evacuate from the predicted path of the storm. Listen to the radio for advice from the authorities and make sure you heed that advice.

HURRICANES: WHAT TO DO IF IT ALL GOES WRONG

If you find yourself in the path of a hurricane and are unable to evacuate, get indoors, preferably in a cellar or a shelter below ground. If you can't get to such a place, you should secure yourself in a middle room where there are no windows. Get under a sturdy piece of furniture that will shield you if the roof gets blown off. Take a mattress or pillow to protect yourself.

If you have adequate warning of the hazard, you should make sure you have enough emergency supplies to see you through the storm. Bear in mind that it may be days before rescue teams can get to you. For each person you should have enough drinking water for three days as well as three days' worth of non-perishable food. A radio and a torch with spare batteries are also essential, as is a well-stocked first aid kit, including any medications you take.

Bring indoors anything that could become a missile during high winds. This could include things like garden furniture and tools. Board up doors and windows. Set your fridge to the coldest setting, as power will likely be lost and this will help to preserve the food for longer. If the place where you are staying has a bath tub, fill it with water so that you have an additional supply.

If you find yourself in a high-rise building or multi-storey hotel, in case of flooding move above the third floor. Do not go above the tenth floor, as the winds will be more intense at this level. If you are in a mobile home or caravan-type dwelling, you need to get to a more robust structure. Similarly, if you are on a flood plain or low-lying land, you must get to higher ground and seek shelter there.

Before the storm hits, unplug all electrical appliances and turn off gas supplies. If you lose power during the storm, keep circuit breakers switched off until power is restored.

Monitor events on the radio and don't leave your shelter until local authorities say it is safe to do so. Remember that a lull in the hurricane could indicate that the eye of the storm is directly over you. Do not be tempted to leave your place of safety.

Once the storm has passed, exercise extreme caution when leaving your shelter. Downed power lines and gas leaks are genuine hazards, as is flooding.

VOLCANOES: IMPROVING THE ODDS

The ability to predict volcanic activity has improved considerably in recent years. However, Mother Nature can still be highly unpredictable and catch us by surprise. There are over 1,500 active volcanoes on the planet and over 500 million people live near one, so the chance of one erupting near a human settlement is higher than you might think. When they do erupt it can be with lethal force. Large eruptions can be 500 times more powerful than a nuclear bomb, and that's not something anyone wants to be near.

During an eruption, the combination of gases, lava and debris hurtling through the air creates a potentially deadly cocktail. In some cases, melted snow and ice are added to the mix, which creates mudflows, known as lahars, which can reach speeds of over 90 miles (145km) per hour.

The obvious option here, as with hurricanes, is to take full advantage of early warning systems, evacuate at the first opportunity and move to a safe distance.

VOLCANOES: WHAT TO DO IF IT ALL GOES WRONG

There are a number of steps you can take to increase your chances of getting out alive if you are unlucky enough to be caught off guard.

If you are out in the open, make sure you protect your head from falling debris. Place a wet cloth over your nose and mouth so that you don't inhale volcanic ash. If possible, head for an area below a ridge line, as this may offer some protection. Find shelter as quickly as you can and seal all doors, windows, chimneys and vents. Place wet towels beneath the doors.

If your escape route is blocked by lava flow, assess how fast it is running. If the lava flow is slow, you might try to outrun it. However, never run across an active lava flow, as you are likely to get trapped by other flows.

And never try to outrun a lahar: you will always lose. Instead head for higher ground, avoiding canyons and river valleys. Lahars are often preceded by a loud roar, so listen out.

It is also worth noting that ash will do untold damage if it is sucked into a vehicle engine. If you have to drive to escape the volcano, don't exceed 35 miles (56km) per hour.

TSUNAMIS: IMPROVING THE ODDS

Tsunamis occur when there is an earthquake below the surface of the sea that causes large waves. When the waves reach shallow water, they can rise considerably higher than normal and bring about catastrophic damage, which means that coastal regions are the most at risk. There is no tsunami season. A tsunami can be triggered just a few minutes after an earthquake but they can occur at any time, and the danger can still exist long after the initial quake.

The 2004 Boxing Day tsunami awakened the world to the destructive potential of this powerful force of nature. Such was its devastating effect that, through one natural disaster, over 230,000 people across 14 countries lost their lives. That's the equivalent of the population of a city the size of Southampton in the UK.

I was leading an expedition in Iceland when news of the tsunami started to come through and the sheer scale of it was hard to grasp. The fact that it affected communities from Indonesia all the way to the east coast of the African continent seemed hard to believe, but then it was travelling at speeds of up to 500 miles (800km) per hour.

Thankfully, since that event, tsunami early warning systems in our oceans have improved and many countries have clearly marked tsunami evacuation routes in coastal towns and villages.

If you are in an 'at risk' coastal region, plan your evacuation route in advance and actually travel the route to make sure you are familiar with it. You should also have a couple of contingency routes up your sleeve in case your preferred option becomes blocked or impassable.

TSUNAMIS: WHAT TO DO IF IT ALL GOES WRONG

Familiarise yourself with the natural warning signs. These could include an earthquake or any noticeable and rapid rise or fall in sea level. If you become aware of an imminent event or a tsunami alarm, immediately head for higher ground. Don't wait for someone to tell you to do so or for official confirmation that a tsunami is on the way. This warning may come too late. Leave your possessions behind. They will only slow you down and are unlikely to be of much use.

If you can't get to high ground, go to the upper floor or roof of a strong building. As a last resort, if you are caught on low-lying ground climb a tree – the sturdier the better. In the Chilean tsunami of 1960, a man called Ramón Ramírez survived by climbing a Cypress tree and clinging on as the waters of the tsunami rushed by below him.

As a last resort, climb on to something that floats. You have more chance of surviving on something buoyant than if you are completely exposed to nature. There are frequently stories of people who survive tsunamis by clinging to floating objects.

Do not return to the coast until after you have received the official all-clear. There is often more than one tsunami wave and the following waves are regularly bigger than the first one. Tsunamis can last for several hours.

NATURAL DISASTERS CHECKLIST

- Develop an emergency response or evacuation plan. Put together a survival kit, which should contain water, a torch and a radio with spare batteries, emergency water filter and easy-to-carry food rations such as energy bars and dried foods. If you have special dietary requirements, make sure you have extra supplies.
- Have a well-stocked first aid kit and essential medicines, as well as a change of clothes, windproof and waterproof clothing, sturdy shoes, blankets or sleeping bags, and dust masks. Your toiletries should include a towel, soap, toothbrush, sanitary items and toilet paper.

- Remember that after most natural disasters there will often be much devastation and debris. You may not be able to return to your accommodation, so as part of your contingency planning you should find out where you can stay temporarily until things return to normal.

CHAPTER SIX

MEDICAL ISSUES

While international travel is a great way to open your mind to new cultures and ways of living, it can also expose you to diseases you've never come across. As always, preparedness is key, and the best way to stay healthy is to do your research before you go. There is a huge range of immunisations and vaccines available to ensure good health during and after your trip, and which will protect you and your community on your return from any bugs you've inadvertently picked up.

There is a great deal of information online about the various options available, with breakdowns of recommendations for each country. If you are unsure about anything, though, it is well worth seeking medical advice before you set off. Also bear in mind that some people are more vulnerable to infection than others, while some vaccinations can't be given to people with certain medical conditions. There are also some diseases that can't be vaccinated against.

In recent times we have seen viruses like Ebola and Zika make headline news as they have swept through certain parts of the world. It's therefore vital that you check on the latest advice: organisations like Centers for Disease Control and Prevention, or CDC (www. cdc.gov), and The National Travel Health Network and Centre, or NaTHNaC (www.nathnac.net), are great places to start.

The most common infectious illness to affect travellers is diarrhoea, which is mainly caused by food- and water-borne agents. While stomach upsets are part and parcel of travel to some areas of the world, it's worth speaking to your doctor before you go to see whether they will prescribe you an antibiotic for such eventualities. Make sure you tell your doctor exactly where you are going as in certain regions some bacteria have developed a resistance to antibiotics. Also, make sure you dispose of unwanted or unused antibiotics properly and don't just flush them down the toilet. That's one way in which bacteria develop resistance.

Do bear in mind, though, that many stomach upsets are entirely preventable by following good personal hygiene practice and taking care what you eat and drink. It is impossible to safeguard against every possible malady but, with a few sensible precautions, you will put yourself in a strong position.

MY STORY

Before leaving the UK for Vietnam in the early nineties, I spent a lot of time talking about the precautions I needed to take, not only with my GP but also with a medical professional specialising in travel. Vietnam had only recently opened up to the outside world following the years of isolation since the end of the Vietnam War in 1975. The health system in the country was basic to say the least, and therefore it was imperative that I and my long-term travelling companion, Mav, had all the right inoculations and a comprehensive medical kit, including a number of prescription drugs.

The anti-malarial drug recommended by my doctor was mefloquine, which is sometimes referred to by its brand name of Lariam. At the time it was widely regarded as the most effective anti-malarial drug on the market.

From the time I took the first dose, I started to feel some of the side effects, and they weren't particularly enjoyable. My sleep was disturbed and included very realistic nightmares that felt more like hallucinations than dreams, and I would often wake up to find my bed clothes drenched in sweat. I would also suffer bouts of feeling pretty low. I wouldn't go so far as to say I was suffering from depression, but I certainly wasn't feeling myself.

About three weeks into our trip we arrived in Nha Trang, which was in those days a small coastal town that had formerly been the site of a huge US military base during the Vietnam War.

Mav wanted to go diving so we found a dive school and made the necessary arrangements. The school was part owned by a British couple, and after a day of diving we arranged to meet up for beers with a few others who had been on the boat, including Julie who was co-owner of the dive school.

I got talking to Julie and it transpired that, prior to coming to Southeast Asia, she had worked in Kenya. She mentioned that while she was in Kenya she had contracted malaria. It was then that I told her that we had been taking mefloquine.

She looked at me quizzically and said quietly, 'Have you had any side effects?'

I admitted I had been having nightmares and feeling down.

'You need to get off that stuff. It's poison and it can really mess you up,' she said. 'It's just not worth it. I've had malaria and I've also suffered the side effects of mefloquine, and I can tell you now that I would rather have malaria any day than suffer the side effects of that drug.'

She explained that, even after she had stopped taking the mefloquine, she had experienced a quite severe depression that had lasted for months.

I didn't want to get malaria, but I also knew that this drug was having a serious effect on me. I decided at that point that I was no longer going to take it and instead would be a lot more thorough about preventing mosquito bites. This meant wearing long trousers and long-sleeved shirts at dawn, at dusk and into the night; making sure I was covered in the mosquito repellent DEET; and sleeping under a mosquito net. I even used DEET as an aftershave once but it burned so much that I never did it again. Lesson learnt.

I told Mav what I was doing, and while he understood my decision, he said that he would carry on taking mefloquine as he wasn't experiencing any side effects.

For about six months after stopping the mefloquine, I continued to have nights of disturbed sleep and nightmares, but they weren't as bad as when I was on the drug and the episodes became fewer and further between.

A few years later I went to Tanzania to lead an expedition to the summit of Kilimanjaro. I arrived before the rest of the group in order to recce the route and some of the other options available while we were in Tanzania, such as bush walks and safaris. I also took some time to do some of my own exploring, as this was my first trip to Africa.

I spent the next few weeks travelling around Tanzania and using my hotel, The Mountain Inn in Moshi, as a base where I could leave kit and come back to after my travels.

About ten days before the expedition group arrived, I began my recce of Kilimanjaro. The expedition was taking the Machame route, and since there were no huts on this route, this meant that we would be camping and would have to take everything with us, helped by a team of porters.

I was greeted by my guide, who was a local chap from Moshi called Moses. Although Moses was only 27 years old, he had been working on the mountain for over ten years and had worked his way up from porter to head guide. I had decided to carry my own food and equipment for the duration of our time on the mountain and Moses had made arrangements for us to get water along the route.

The first part of the trek was through quite dense forest, and as we were just coming out of the rainy season, the track was just thick mud. Sometimes we would sink up to our knees in the stuff, so the going on that first day was quite slow. By the time we reached the place where we would be camping, everything was caked in mud. We spent a good few hours cleaning our kit before having an evening meal and heading for bed.

Moses told me not to leave anything outside my tent, as some of the other porters were known to be somewhat light-fingered. I took heed of his warning and slept soundly. I always do when I'm camping.

The next morning, just as the sun was making an appearance over the horizon, I was awoken by shouting. One of the tourists from a German group had left his boots inside the outer sheet of his tent but outside the sleeping compartment. When he had awoken his boots were gone, and he was understandably quite upset, as boots are a pretty essential piece of kit for climbing Kili.

The head guides, including Moses, gathered all the porters together and searched through the bags they were carrying. In one of them they found hidden a pair of boots. After the German had identified them as his, the porter responsible for that bag was taken off by the others and beaten. It was pretty rough justice and he was in a bad way by the time they had finished with him.

He pleaded that the boots had been planted there by someone else, but that didn't stop him getting a hiding. He was told to leave the mountain, and the authorities at the entrance were notified by radio that he should be arrested. Kilimanjaro is a massive source of income for the towns around it and the authorities are well aware that, if tourists are robbed while trying to climb it, others will be deterred from making the trip.

The next few days on Kili were fine and there were some spectacular views to enjoy along the way. On the evening of day four, however, I wasn't feeling great so I went to bed early.

By the time I awoke on day five, I was feeling distinctly odd. At first I thought it was my body adjusting to the altitude, but I had experienced acute mountain sickness (AMS) when I was in the Andes and this wasn't it. I was running a fever but was also freezing cold. My limbs were aching and I was shivering.

Moses took one look at me and said, 'Oh, Mr Lloyd, you are not very well. We need to get you back to Moshi and fast.'

Before I knew it, my tent was packed up and a porter from one of the tour groups was seconded to carry my kit back down the mountain.

On a mountain like Kili, going down is usually much easier than climbing up, but every step was a strain. By the time Moses, the porter and I got back to our first campsite, where the German had had his boots stolen, I knew I was in a bad way. My joints had teamed up with my limbs in the aching stakes and I was now simultaneously burning up with fever and shivering as though I had hypothermia. My vision was becoming blurred and I knew that if I sat down I would never get up again.

Moses was starting to look very concerned.

'Mr Lloyd, we need to get you to the doctor straight away,' he said. 'You are very sick.'

Tell me about it, I thought, but all I could do was to grunt back at him. I had to concentrate with all my might just to put one foot in front of the other.

After what seemed an eternity we reached the end of the trail and Saleem, the manager of The Mountain Inn in Moshi, was waiting for us in a Land Rover. Moses must have radioed ahead. I had to be helped into the front seat and Saleem immediately sped off.

Eventually we pulled up outside a small building and I saw a sign that read: 'Welcome to the Shanty Town Clinic'.

Oh bugger; that didn't look good.

I asked Saleem whether there wasn't a better place to go and he assured me that this was the best doctor in town.

Before we went in I told Saleem that I must have the first aid kit from my bag and he duly obliged in getting it. I knew that they would want to take a blood sample and I had a set of sterile needles and syringes with me. I told Saleem that they could only take blood from me using my needles and that he had to make sure of this. He agreed, and I was placed on a bed in a corridor.

I must have slept or passed out, I don't know which or for how long, but when I awoke there was a nurse sticking a needle in my arm and taking blood. Saleem, who was standing next to her, assured me she was using a needle and a syringe from my first aid kit. Everything went blurry and then I was out again.

The next thing I remember was being taken into a room that looked more like a headmaster's study than a doctor's consulting room. There was a desk with a chair either side, and a bookcase, but my vision was too blurred to read any of the titles of the books. There was also a medicine cabinet on the other side of the room.

The nurse left me there alone, slumped in a chair, and after what seemed like an age the door opened and a man in a white coat entered. He didn't say anything but took his place behind the desk and then went through a ritual of putting a stethoscope around his neck and perching a pair of glasses on the end of his nose. He then looked over the top of his glasses, directly at me.

Finally, he broke the silence: 'Mr Figgins, you have malaria.'

He sounded almost proud of his diagnosis. It was only then that I saw the nurse was standing by the desk, and she too was looking very pleased with the doctor's diagnosis.

'No, it can't be malaria,' I said. 'I have an expedition to lead up Kilimanjaro in less than a week, so I can't have malaria.'

This really was going to put a spanner in the works.

The doctor looked over his glasses again and repeated his diagnosis. I was handed a box of tablets and told to get plenty of rest. With that the nurse ushered me out of the room.

Saleem was waiting for me outside and he took me to the Land Rover.

'I've got malaria, Saleem,' I said as he put me in the vehicle.

'I know,' he replied.

'Did the doctor speak to you?'

'No, I knew the second I saw you come off the mountain. We have a lot of malaria here and we see it often.'

Saleem told me that he would give me a room at The Mountain Inn for as long as I needed it for my recovery. He said he'd get one of the members of staff, Joseph, to visit my room regularly to check whether I was OK.

I then called the expedition company headquarters in the UK and told them what had happened.

'Well, get some rest and you should be all right to meet the group in Nairobi in a few days,' came the reply, but their response didn't register with me and I just went to bed.

I don't remember much after that. I have no idea how long I slept or whether it was day or night, but by the time I awoke I knew I was very sick indeed. Every movement was painful and I was drenched in sweat, as was my bed. The simultaneous fever and shivering had continued, and to make it worse I also had a serious case of gastroenteritis. I was so weak that I could barely stand and had to summon all my strength when I needed to get to the toilet. By the time I made it back to my bed I was exhausted.

Joseph came in with fresh drinking water and insisted I drank some, but every time I did it set off another race to the toilet. Then I'd pass out again and sleep.

And sleep wasn't normal sleep. It was very fitful, and there were times when I couldn't tell the difference between being asleep and being awake. I was starting to hallucinate, and on one occasion everyone who came into my room had their own bodies but the face of my father. This was extremely odd, particularly seeing as most people there were black and my father was white. Joseph came in to bring me water and spoke to me in his own voice, but his face was that of my dad.

Saleem told me that the expedition company had hired an additional head guide to take my place on the ascent of Kili but still wanted me to travel to Nairobi to meet the team and escort them back to Moshi. He had tried to explain to them that I was very ill and not in any condition to travel anywhere, but they said there was no alternative.

The next day, I crawled out of my bed, took six Imodium tablets to control my gastroenteritis for the eight-hour journey to Nairobi and boarded the tourist bus back to the Kenyan capital. I have no recollection of that journey.

When we got to Nairobi, I was woken by one of my fellow travellers, an American chap.

'Dude, I don't think you're very well,' he said.

'It's all right – I just have a touch of malaria,' I replied.

He shook his head and helped me off the bus and into a taxi to my hotel. I checked in and collapsed in my room.

The next morning, I met the driver of the transport company that was taking the group from Nairobi to Moshi. We went to the airport to meet the group. The driver could see I was in a bad way so he volunteered to go inside the airport to gather the group while I slept in the bus.

Once we had everyone on board, I popped another large dose of Imodium, explained to the group that I wouldn't be accompanying them up the mountain as I was rather unwell, and informed them that the journey to Moshi would take about eight hours. I then curled up and went back to sleeping, sweating and shivering.

By the time we got to Moshi, I had deteriorated further and the group seemed genuinely concerned for me. I gave everyone a safety briefing and their room keys and then went back to my own room and hoped the end would come soon.

The experience of malaria is difficult to describe. Try

imagining the worst flu you have ever had (man flu doesn't count), multiplying that by 10, and adding gastroenteritis and hallucinations: that isn't even close to what it feels like.

I don't know how long I was out but there are certainly three or four days of which I have no recollection. Those are days I will never get back and for that I am grateful.

The pain and discomfort were soul-destroying and I became so weak that I had to be helped to the toilet by Joseph and then helped back to my bed. I could no longer raise my head off my sodden pillow without experiencing great pain. All I wanted was my mum to look after me.

More days passed – I don't know how many – and then one day, on a rare occasion that I was awake, the door of my room burst open and there stood someone I recognised. Was I hallucinating?

It was Jamie Henderson, a larger-than-life character who had trained with me as an expedition leader. We had always got along well and shared a similar sense of humour. As well as being an all-round good bloke, Henderson was also the poshest man I had ever met. In fact, I found out many years later that in his school yearbook he had been described by his classmates as being 'posher than the Queen'. It was an accurate description.

Was he really there now, standing in the doorway of my hotel room? Henderson was a bit of an Africa specialist, so it made sense that he could be in the area.

'Now then, Figgins old chum, what's all this I hear about you having malaria?' he said. 'Can't have that, old boy, it's simply not on. Come along – let's get you sorted out.'

It was Henderson all right.

He proceeded to run me a shower and then told Joseph to get one of the housemaids to change my sheets. He led me to the shower cubicle, made sure the water was the right temperature and then stuck me in it along with a bar of soap.

'Now have a good wash, Figgins, there's a good chap. Not to

put too fine a point on it but you are a bit ripe. How long have you been like this?'

I thought about it but honestly didn't know.

Once I had got out of the shower, Henderson handed me a razor and some shaving foam.

'Can't have you looking like a navvy, Figgins. You'll feel better after a shave and I'll let you have some of my Calvin Klein aftershave to make you smell a bit better.'

Only Henderson would go around the African bush with a bottle of Calvin Klein cologne. At least I knew for certain I wasn't hallucinating now.

Once I had washed and shaved, Henderson got me into some clean clothes and refused to allow me to get back into bed.

'No point lounging around here any longer, Figgins. Looks like you've done enough of that. What on earth were you thinking, catching malaria?'

He had a point: it wasn't the best thing I had ever done.

'When was the last time you had some grub?'

'I'm not sure, Henderson – it's all been a bit of a blur.'

'Right, well we need to fix that, old bean. You've lost a lot of weight, so we need to feed you back up.'

We went to the hotel bar and sat outside on the veranda. I wasn't even asked what I wanted. Henderson summoned the waiter and ordered chicken burgers with chips for us both. I wasn't hungry but was too tired to argue.

The food arrived and I nibbled at a few chips. They tasted good. Before I knew it I was chomping into the burger, and it too tasted delicious.

'Best chicken burger in all of East Africa!' Henderson exclaimed. 'Just as well, because the rest of their menu is bloody awful.'

Henderson and I chatted into the evening and he told me all about his adventures in Africa, including the time he was convinced he was going to be eaten by a hyena.

As the sun set, Henderson turned to me and said, 'Figgins, when was the last time you had a cold beer?'

'I can't remember. Must have been before I went up the mountain.'

Henderson looked concerned and turned to the waiter to order two bottles of Kibo Gold, which was the popular local brew of Moshi. Beer was the last thing I wanted, but the first sip tasted like heaven and it didn't take long before Henderson was ordering two more.

After the second beer it was time for me to head back to my room. It had been an exhausting day but Henderson had brought some much-needed cheer to my miserable existence.

The next morning I awoke and wandered down to the veranda, where I had agreed to meet Henderson. He was there reading a copy of *The Times*, drinking a cup of coffee and looking every bit the quintessential Brit. God only knows where he had managed to get *The Times* in the middle of the African bush.

When I told him I was feeling much better, he clapped his hands together, sat back in his lounge chair and exclaimed, 'I knew it! I knew that Kibo Gold would sort you out. We may well have discovered the cure for malaria there.'

To this day Henderson reminds me that the cure for malaria is indeed Kibo Gold.

I remained in Tanzania for another week or so before flying back to the UK. I saw my doctor as soon as I got home and explained about my experience. He took blood samples to be sent off for analysis. There wasn't going to be time for me to get the results before I headed off on my next expedition, which was a crossing of the Karakum Desert between Turkmenistan and Uzbekistan.

I did show my GP the medication the doctor at the Shanty Town Clinic had given me, but he could find no record of the brand and therefore advised me to stop taking it. He was worried that it might not have undergone the usual clinical testing that would be expected by western medics. God knows what I had been taking during those weeks in Tanzania.

I felt under the weather throughout the time I was in Central Asia, but I managed to complete my next expedition in one piece.

However, by the time I got back to Ashgabat, the capital of Turkmenistan, it was obvious that the malaria had resurfaced. I spent two days shaking, sweating and shivering in my hotel room and was very pleased to be getting out of the country.

Within a week of getting back from Turkmenistan, I was heading out to lead an expedition across the Sierra Madre mountains in Mexico so once again my health took a back seat. The blood tests had come back from the hospital as 'inconclusive' and so there was now some doubt over the diagnosis given by the doctor in Tanzania.

The trek across the Mexican mountains was stunning and had the bonus of ending up in the Pacific coastal town of Puerto Escondido. It was a great place to end an expedition, but by the time I got there I was feeling very unwell again.

This time I was lucky that two British medics were part of the expedition. Doctors Ruth Marchant and Fiona Cowan could see that I was pretty sick and convinced me that I had to return to the UK to get proper medical treatment.

I called the expedition company HQ in the UK and again they were less than sympathetic. They reminded me that I had more expeditions to lead in Mexico, Guatemala and Belize and that my returning home would leave them in the lurch. I didn't want to do that but I was finding it very hard to function. Eventually, Ruth and Fiona stepped in and told me (and the expedition company) that if I didn't get immediate medical help I would risk permanently damaging my health, or worse.

The expedition company remained stubborn, but within a few days I was on a flight back to the UK (which the company refused to pay for) and had an appointment to visit the Hospital for Tropical Diseases in London.

On the day of the appointment I felt better than I had in months but they took every sample they could from me, as well as a comprehensive history of where I had been. By the end of that year (1999) I had travelled to 18 countries, so they had their work cut out to determine where I had caught whatever it was that was causing me so much misery.

They also told me that it would be very useful for me to come back to them when I was actually in fever. I had been given a temporary role by the expedition company at their headquarters, which was only a 50-minute train journey from London. I assured the doctors that the next time I felt the symptoms coming on I would jump on a train.

In January 2000, I was working in the office when I started to feel the now all too familiar symptoms. I spoke to my boss and explained what I needed to do and she was very understanding.

As I walked down to the train station, I could feel the sweating starting to get worse. By the time I got on the train to London, the shivering had started, and once I reached the capital my symptoms were in full swing.

I got on a tube train and sat down. I was now sweating profusely, shaking rather violently and hugging myself because I felt so cold. I had noticed during previous episodes that my skin would go very pale and clammy, and therefore it was no surprise that no one wanted to sit near me. In fact it's probably the only time I have had a whole tube carriage to myself during London rush hour. The other travellers huddled like sardines by the doors rather than get closer than necessary to this quivering, sweating wreck of a man.

I got off the tube and struggled to walk the short distance to the hospital. When I arrived the medical staff looked very excited to have a patient in full fever arrive on their doorstep and I was immediately admitted.

Over the course of that evening and the following day they conducted a series of tests, and at the end of it they were able to confirm that I did, in fact, have malaria. They were confident, however, that they could successfully treat it. I was given a course of medication and discharged the next day.

They were somewhat surprised that I hadn't sought help sooner and that I had been able to lead the expeditions I had in such a debilitated condition. I was ordered to rest and to let my body recover.

Of course, I probably wouldn't have caught malaria in the first place if I had been taking anti-malarial medication, but after my experience with mefloquine in Vietnam I had thrown the dice and lost. It was the wrong thing to do and the result was not good. It was also a wake-up call to me that my health is the most important thing I have, particularly when travelling. Since that time, I have been religious in ensuring I am as protected as I possibly can be whenever and wherever I travel. I was lucky in many respects, but others have not been and have suffered far more severe consequences as a result.

As a footnote to this story, back in July 2013 the US Food and Drug Administration (FDA) issued a 'black box' safety warning for mefloquine. It recognised that the drug is neurotoxic and can cause permanent injury to the brainstem and emotional centres in the limbic system. Mefloquine has been linked to lasting neurological and psychiatric problems, including a number of suicides. However, despite calls to end its use in Britain too, at the time of writing it is still being prescribed to British soldiers.

IMPROVING THE ODDS

All travellers should be sure to get the latest advice from their doctor or health clinic before they travel. Your doctor will have the most up-to-date information on disease and disease prevention. It's always worth doing this plenty of time in advance.

In addition, it's well worth investing in a first aid qualification that is relevant to the type of travel you are planning on undertaking. A traditional urban 'first aid at work' course is not going to equip you with the skills and knowledge required for a jungle or mountain expedition. Wilderness-specific courses are going to be much more useful if you or one of your party gets into trouble.

Put together a comprehensive first aid kit to take with you and, again, make sure it is tailored to the environments in which you are going to be travelling. The off-the-shelf kits you can buy in outdoor shops and chemists are limited. You will be far better off putting together your own kit: that way you will know exactly what's in it and where to find each item. A 'giving kit' of sterile needles and syringes is essential in countries where sanitised medical facilities are not the norm.

If a doctor prescribes medication, be sure to take the full course. Many medicines require that you continue to take them even after you have returned home. Make sure you do this. A lot of people think that, simply because they are home, they are safe. This is not the case.

It is vital that you have adequate and appropriate insurance for your trip. This should include comprehensive cover for medical expenses, repatriation and any legal costs. Often the travel insurance policies you get free with a credit card or bank account don't offer very comprehensive cover, and neither do the cheaper travel policies. There's a reason these policies are free or cheap and you don't want to be finding that out at a time when you might need help the most.

There are a number of measures you should take when you are actually travelling. These will significantly increase your odds of staying in good health.

Always practise good personal hygiene and make sure others in your group do the same. This includes thoroughly washing your hands after going to the toilet and before handling food. I always have plenty of anti-bacterial hand wash on my expeditions and make sure that everyone uses it.

Drink plenty of water and avoid alcohol, caffeine and soft drinks, as all of these will dehydrate you, especially in hot climates or at altitude. Be sure that the water you drink is clean and has been appropriately purified. It's best to drink bottled water where it's available, and make sure that the top is sealed. Don't put ice in your drinks or eat the local ice cream, especially if you are in a place subject to frequent power cuts. Ice preserves germs; it doesn't kill them.

Avoid food that hasn't been thoroughly cooked throughout, as well as uncooked food that you can't peel, including salad and fruit. If food has been washed as part of the preparation process, make sure that the water used to wash it is of drinkable quality.

Buffets can be a breeding ground for germs as the food often consists of leftovers that have been gently reheated, creating the perfect conditions for germs to flourish. Ever wondered about those stories where everyone at a wedding goes down with food poisoning and why that happens? Well, now you know.

WHAT TO DO IF IT ALL GOES WRONG

If you develop symptoms while travelling, such as diarrhoea, high fever or flu-like illness, see a doctor right away. Tell the doctor treating you where you have been, what medications you are on, any allergies you have, your past medical history and your symptoms.

If you feel you need further assistance, you may need to contact your insurance company, as they will likely have agreements in place with certain hospitals and can arrange for payment of your treatment and, in a worst-case scenario, to have you repatriated. If no other help is available, contact your embassy or consulate.

Be sure to have a plan in place to enable you to get to the best medical facility quickly. You should have an emergency evacuation plan for each leg of your journey that details hospitals, clinics and doctors. Make sure you share this with someone at home so that they will know where you are likely to go in an emergency.

MEDICAL ISSUES CHECKLIST

- Stay hydrated by drinking bottled water and don't miss out on sleep. Both are effective weapons against becoming ill and help fight off illness if you are already infected.
- If you have medication that works well for you when you are ill, take it with you on your trip. It can be really challenging when travelling to obtain the kinds of medicines that are available over the counter at home. Moreover, what seems to be the same medicine can have a different formula in different parts of the world. If there's also a potential language barrier, it can be hard to know exactly what you are getting.
- If you do fall ill, you may be inclined to let your body try to fight off the bacteria for a while. However, if there are no signs of the symptoms subsiding, you would be advised to seek help sooner rather than later. Many conditions are caused by bacteria that are strong and/or unfamiliar to your body and need urgent medical intervention. Your condition will be much harder to treat if it is allowed to develop to a dangerous level.
- Make sure that, if things get really serious, you have a plan for getting home and an insurance policy that will facilitate your repatriation.
- If you become ill once you are back home, make sure that you tell your doctor that you have been overseas and list the countries

and regions you have visited, even if your illness develops months after your return.

- If you are undertaking a major expedition to a remote region, it's worth engaging the services of a doctor, paramedic or emergency medical technician as expedition medic. Ideally everyone on the team should have a wilderness first aid qualification, but if this is not possible, there should be at least two people thus qualified, in case one becomes ill or injured.

- If you are overseas on business, find out if your employer has a contract with a specialist medical assistance provider. If so, ask what services they provide as well as how to contact them in the event of an emergency. These companies can provide over-the-phone medical advice, as well as assistance in getting you to the right hospital and, if required, repatriated.

Growing up, my elder brother Mike was instrumental in getting me to push boundaries. This often ended badly for me.

Moments before setting off to take on Devil's Hill. Note the lack of any safety equipment.

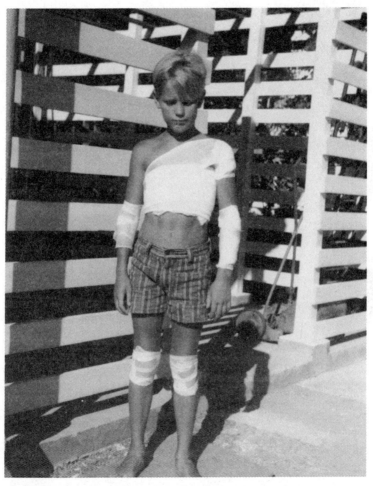

The aftermath of my Devil's Hill adventure. Mike's challenges often ended in a trip to the hospital for me.

Mario and Lionel, our Colombian guides into the jungle.

Trekking deep into the Colombian jungle with my good friend Maverick.

Halfway up Kilimanjaro. The next day I was struck down with what turned out to be Malaria.

Crossing the Sinai desert in Egypt in 2002. Travel comes with many challenges so the right skills and knowledge are essential.

Local Cambodian transport in rural Ratanakiri Province, before I headed to the busier roads and experienced the traffic accident described in Chapter Seven.

Local woman in Ratanakiri, Cambodia. Some of the friendliest people I've met have next to nothing, but are willing to share what little they do have.

Palmyra the day before the attack described in Chapter Ten.

CHAPTER SEVEN

VEHICLE SAFETY

Of all the hazards we face while travelling, far and away the one most likely to lead to injury is a vehicle-related incident. Very often, though, these are entirely preventable.

When I run travel-safety workshops, I always ask how many of the audience put on a seat belt when getting into a vehicle in their home country. Without fail everyone raises their hand, and some even look at me as if the question I've just asked is rather stupid. However, when I ask the same group how many of them wear a seat belt when they travel abroad, fewer than half raise a hand. And when I ask how many would refuse to travel in a vehicle that wasn't equipped with seat belts, I'm often on my own.

I am amazed that so many people, when travelling abroad, simply don't feel the need to protect themselves and preserve their own safety in the way they would in their home country – despite the fact that, in many cases, the countries they're visiting have lower standards of road safety and higher rates of road fatalities. I can only assume that they inadvertently lower their guard because they associate being abroad with positive experiences. Or maybe they view poorer safety standards as being part of the romance of travel – a 'when in Rome' mindset, perhaps?

If you find yourself in this group, statistics from the World Health

Organization may change your mind. They certainly paint a pretty worrying picture of which any traveller, whether on business or for pleasure, should be aware:

- Road traffic crashes kill 1.2 million people a year or an average of 3,242 people every day.
- Road traffic crashes injure or disable between 20 and 50 million people a year.
- Road traffic crashes account for 2.1 per cent of all deaths globally.

The majority of deaths from road traffic crashes (90 per cent) occur in low- and middle-income countries. Many of these are the same countries to which western tourists and business people commonly travel. And despite increasing awareness of vehicle safety, the problem is actually getting worse. According to the Global Burden of Diseases, Injuries, and Risk Factors Study, road traffic accidents – which currently rank ninth in the cause-of-death league table – are set to rise to fifth by 2030, overtaking diseases such as cancer, diabetes, hypertensive heart disease and HIV/AIDS. While treatment and care for common diseases is, of course, improving all the time, road traffic accidents still represent an ongoing danger.

It's not just cars and buses either. Many travellers think nothing of renting a motorcycle or moped when abroad, yet these machines are responsible for a huge number of tourist deaths every year. According to the British Foreign & Commonwealth Office, 38 people die each day in motorcycle crashes in Thailand alone. So taking into consideration just one mode of transport in a single country, that's nearly 14,000 people a year.

There are always times in life when we don't have choices, but when it comes to transport and travel, we often do, and our choices here could literally mean the difference between life and death.

While tour operators and employers have a moral and legal responsibility for our safety, their decisions can be governed by motives of profit rather than wellbeing. Ultimately, it is up to us as individuals to ensure that whatever mode of transport we take complies with acceptable levels of safety. If it doesn't, refuse to use it. You owe it to yourself to speak up and demand safe transportation.

MY STORY

In the year 2000 I was working in Cambodia, a fascinating country but one not without its issues following the tyrannical regime of Pol Pot and the Khmer Rouge in the 1970s. By 2000 the capital, Phnom Penh, was beginning to show the first signs of western influence, but just like Vietnam when I first went there, tourism was really still in its infancy.

Although they had long been ousted, a significant contributory factor in this was the pockets of Khmer Rouge that still existed in certain parts of the country. There was also a large number of unexploded ordnance (UXOs), particularly in the more rural areas. Reminders of this were everywhere and the number of amputees in the country was striking: it seemed utterly disproportionate that those who had been maimed by mines appeared to be in the majority. As a result of the risks from the Khmer Rouge and UXOs, the few tourists who got to Cambodia tended to visit Phnom Penh and Siem Reap and then get out as quickly as they could.

I wanted to see the real Cambodia, so I flew to the northeast province of Ratanakiri, where the Khmer Rouge had built their regional base in the 1960s. The region had also been subject to heavy American military bombardment during the Vietnam War, so the residents had had a tough time.

Ratanakiri is one of the poorest and least populated areas of the country, and its people are mostly subsistence farmers. Nevertheless, just as I'd experienced in other parts of the world, once they got to know me they were very hospitable and generous.

Given that there were no paved roads in the area and that I would be travelling at slow speeds along the jungle dirt tracks that connected the remote communities, a motorbike seemed the best – and safest – option. It would give me the freedom to explore and was certainly safer than travelling on some of the local buses I'd seen.

I didn't want too big a bike, as I realised that I would have to get off and push it through some of the muddier sections of my journey, but I did need something that was up to the task. I found a local second-hand dealer and bought a Honda that had seen better days but would certainly do the trick. I tied my rucksack to the back and set off.

Although it's a mode of transport that makes you very vulnerable, there's a real sense of freedom to riding a motorbike and I loved the thrill of it.

In every village I stopped at, I was first greeted by an elder, after which a conversation in sign language would ensue before I was allowed to look around and join the elders for refreshment, usually tea of some kind.

The children would be the next to welcome me, and once they had got over their initial fear of a man with pale skin and blond hair, they would often tug at the light-coloured hairs on my forearms and laugh. Some would stroke the hairs on my arms as if I were a pet. It was all very amusing, although it could be painful if a child decided to try and yank out my hair in search of a souvenir.

I was always offered food and they would never accept payment. When I arrived at a village near dark, I was invariably offered shelter too. It caused a huge commotion and much hilarity when I set up my roll mat, sleeping sheet and mosquito net in whatever hut they had provided me. I must have looked like a total wimp with all these 'luxury' items while the locals just curled up on the floor and went to sleep. I would often hear the children whispering and giggling uncontrollably, no doubt having a joke at my expense, but it was a lovely sound to drop off to.

I spent the best part of a month with the people in that remote part of the country, and it was some of the most grounding travel I've experienced. There wasn't one village that hadn't been affected by the ravages of war – everywhere there were people who had lost limbs owing to mines or bombs – but these were also some of the happiest people I've ever encountered. My overriding memory is of their smiles and laughter.

By the time I had to return to Phnom Penh, I was sad to leave. I sold my motorbike – at a massive loss – back to the bloke I'd bought it from. He went to great lengths to describe how in recent weeks the bottom had completely dropped out of the market for second-hand motorbikes. Never had he seen such a sharp devaluation! The bike had served me well, however, so I couldn't really begrudge him his profit.

I spent a few days back in the capital catching up with some chores before deciding to head down to the coastal town of Sihanoukville in the southwest of the country on a local bus. Tourist buses and local buses were exactly the same vehicles in those days, the only difference being that the tourist buses were reserved exclusively for tourists and cost five times the price. Still, most tourists were happy (and able) to pay the inflated fares.

The bus left Phnom Penh early in the morning for the six-hour drive to Sihanoukville.

Driving in Cambodia in the early 2000s was a chaotic experience at the best of times, but there's always something exhilarating about seeing a country by road and witnessing at first hand the hustle and bustle of everyday life. However, there's also a danger in travelling in unregulated, poorly maintained vehicles on poorly maintained roads, and the accident I was about to find myself in was in many ways inevitable, given the volume of traffic and the chaos caused by the apparent lack of any road rules.

I didn't see the woman on the motorbike: I just heard a screech of brakes and felt the bus skid sideways towards the oncoming traffic. The bus felt as though it had been skidding for ages before it finally hit something solid. That something solid was another bus that had been travelling in the opposite direction, straight towards us.

From the moment I realised we were skidding until our abrupt halt on collision with the other bus, time seemed to stand still. All the while I felt utterly powerless to do anything to improve the situation. I became very aware that I was not wearing a seat belt (there weren't any) and that therefore, despite my best efforts to hang on for dear life, the force at the point of impact would propel me into whatever object lay in its path.

I was in the middle of the bus and was thrown against the seat in front of me, which thudded into my ribs. The top half of my torso continued over the top of the seat and hit the passenger occupying it. In turn, the passenger behind me flew over my seat and crashed into me, and this sequence was repeated throughout the bus.

By the time I had regained some degree of composure, I was aware that there was screaming all around and people were looking dazed and confused. Fortunately we had been travelling relatively slowly and no one on the bus appeared to be badly injured. There were a number of cuts and bruises but nothing more serious.

Outside the bus was a different story. In developing countries like Cambodia, every road is packed with a combination of motorised vehicles, pedestrians, bicycles and animals, and when the two buses had collided, those not inside the steel cage of the vehicle were the worst affected. It looked like a scene from a war movie. There were bodies all over the place, mostly alive but with some serious injuries.

There was also a water buffalo lying on the side of the road. One of its legs seemed to be broken and it was struggling without success to get back on its feet. The noise it was making was louder than anything coming from the human casualties; my ears were filled with the sound of its bellows. The broken leg, however, had sealed its fate. It was a while, though, before its throat was slit and it finally fell silent.

Observing the pandemonium outside the bus, my gaze was drawn to one young woman in particular. I couldn't take my eyes off her. The motorbike she had been riding lay on top of her left leg but the rest of her looked unharmed, apart from her head. Her face was untouched – you could see that she had been beautiful – but she hadn't been wearing a helmet so the top of her skull had cracked open and she was now lying motionless on the road. When I had rented the motorbike in Ratanakiri I also made sure it came with a helmet and I had to try a few to get one in good condition that fitted correctly. There's no underestimating the importance of wearing a helmet on any type of bike, motorised or not.

What I couldn't disengage from was the child sitting next to her and pulling at her clothing, willing her to be alive. The little girl made no noise but tears streamed down her face. She was probably only four or five years old.

I felt utterly hopeless. I could help treat those who were injured and I started to do so, but there was nothing I could do for this child. I felt somehow ashamed that the bus I'd been travelling on had in some way contributed to the death. I busied myself with helping where I could, but all the time my eyes were drawn back to the little girl and her dead mother.

Eventually a local woman came along and tried to stop her clutching at her mother's dress. It was only then that the child made a sound. As the woman led her away, she screamed for all she was worth. It was one of the saddest things I have ever seen.

In due course the road was cleared of most of the chaos caused by the accident so that normal service could be resumed.

In the end, the only remaining obstacle was the body of the mother, with the motorbike on top of her.

It seemed undignified to leave her lying there like that, so I took a sarong from my bag and covered her until the ambulance arrived to scoop up her broken body and take it away.

My own injuries were minor and took about a week to heal. My ribs hurt for a while and so did my neck and head, owing to the impact with the seat and the passenger in front of me. But on the whole, like everyone else on the bus, I was fine.

For the little girl, however, the horror of that day would last a lifetime: the image of her dead mother, lying on the road, would be indelibly etched into her mind.

IMPROVING THE ODDS

If, as travellers, we continue to accept poor-quality, ill-equipped vehicles driven by unqualified drivers who exceed or ignore speed limits, we are asking for trouble. If, on the other hand, we insist that tour operators and transport companies provide good-quality, well-maintained vehicles with fitted seat belts and qualified drivers who are adequately rested and not under the influence of drink or drugs, we are at least taking steps to decrease the risk.

To give an example, a few years ago I was in charge of risk and security for a team of high-ranking African scientists who were headed to a remote part of Kenya. We had set off from Nairobi later than expected because some of the members of the expedition were not at the departure point on time, and by the time late afternoon came round it was obvious that we wouldn't arrive at our destination before nightfall.

The option of driving deep into the Kenyan bush after dark, with no support, was not an appealing one, so I made the decision to stop for the night at a hotel in the town of Isiolo. Isiolo does not have the best safety record for travellers but I located a hotel that was being used by Médecins Sans Frontières. I had worked with them previously in Cambodia and knew they would have done a risk assessment on the accommodation. There was also a security detail from another organisation staying at the hotel.

The problem was that the hotel only had a limited number of rooms available, which meant that some people would have to share. I got the keys and allocated the rooms.

I made sure that each of the three drivers had their own room and gave them strict instructions that they were not to consume any alcohol and that they were to go to bed early.

They had all driven for nine hours that day, though they took a break every two hours; the previous two weeks had seen them driving for another company for similar amounts of time, though in that case without breaks. They had also been up since four o' clock that morning and were understandably very tired. We all were, but the drivers were the ones who would be responsible for getting us to our destination safely the next day, and therefore I wanted them to be on good form.

They were clearly delighted by the room allocation as they usually slept in their vehicles. Here they had their own rooms and en-suite bathrooms.

The scientists were not so grateful! They were used to being accommodated in the best rooms of any hotel they stayed in and certainly weren't used to sharing, particularly when 'lowly' drivers were given the best accommodation. They wasted little time in venting their discontent on me, so I did what I've done so many times before and since: I bought them all a drink, sat them down and told them the story about looking for lemons. The 'lemons' had been stacking up since we left Nairobi and I explained to the scientists why I had allocated the best rooms to the drivers.

Whilst the vast majority of the scientists understood and accepted my logic in ensuring the drivers were well looked after and rested, one of the group most certainly didn't appreciate my decision. He refused to speak to me for the remainder of the expedition and although he complied with my advice, he was clearly very unhappy. However, this is a common risk management lesson that's worth highlighting. Even if you have the best interests and safety of others at heart, sometimes your decisions will be unpopular. Try not to take it personally and gain some solace in the fact that even if they don't appreciate it, you have probably kept them from harm.

When it comes to vehicle safety, you have to be assertive. We are naturally concerned about speaking to others in a way that might seem insulting or disrespectful, and it takes moral courage to reject a vehicle or driver that for whatever reason seems unsuitable. However, an unwillingness to offend is going to seem like a pretty feeble kind of excuse if you find yourself in a foreign hospital – or worse. I have had to reject vehicles or drivers on safety grounds on more than one occasion and, yes, it has at times made me very unpopular. I would rather deal with the unpopularity, however, than with the aftermath of a crash.

The more people who take a stand and refuse to put lives in danger by turning a blind eye to poor-quality drivers and vehicles, the sooner the message will start to filter through. And as I have seen in other aspects of travel safety, rogue operators go out of business once they are unable to meet the safety requirements and expectations of the paying customer.

Education is equally important. Many people in developing countries simply haven't had the benefit of the training in road safety that we take for granted. Be under no illusion: seat belts save lives. Fact! However, in some countries this seems to be systematically ignored. A study in Kenya showed that 99 per cent of those injured in vehicle crashes were not wearing seat belts, despite the legal requirement that drivers and front-seat passengers should do so.

It's not just a case that those in the front seats should wear seat belts either. When travelling in buses, it only takes one person not wearing a seat belt to effectively create a human missile.

Consider this: a person travelling in a bus moving at 60 miles (100km) per hour is travelling at the same speed as the bus. If the vehicle suddenly stops (as happened in the crash in Cambodia), that person will continue to move at the same speed inside the vehicle. And they will do so until something – the steering wheel, the dashboard, the windshield or another passenger – stops them. They will then collide into whatever object is blocking their path at the same speed as they would hit the pavement after falling from a three-storey building. Being hit by a fellow passenger who weighs, say, 75 kilos (165 pounds) and is travelling inside a vehicle moving at 60 miles per hour is never going to have a positive outcome.

Everyone travelling in a multi-person vehicle has a responsibility to themselves and to their fellow passengers to wear a seat belt. However, it's only if people are made consciously aware of this fact that the message is going to get through. I train organisations to teach their drivers not to turn the ignition key until everyone is wearing a seat belt. It is a very simple technique and it doesn't take long for the idea to sink in: until everyone is belted up, the vehicle just doesn't start.

It's imperative to make local drivers feel like part of the team. Where possible, before starting a journey, and especially if I have chartered the vehicle, I take the driver(s) to one side and give a thorough briefing on my expectations. I explain to them that we have high safety standards and I make it clear that if these are not adhered to we may need to look at alternative providers.

Don't forget that transport companies are going to be very keen to hold on to the business, and if they think there's a chance of you using them on a regular basis, they will comply with your requests. But never be afraid to turn a company down if you have doubts about their ability to provide safe transportation and drivers.

When hiring a driver, a simple checklist to work through with him/her might include:
- Check the vehicle before any journey, including tyres (to ensure that they are properly inflated and that they have sufficient tread), oil, petrol and fluids. Drivers should also check that all the lights, the indicators and the horn are working.

- Ensure that drivers are fully rested before getting behind the wheel and have not consumed any alcohol in the past 24 hours.
- Make sure you check that the driver has a valid licence and the correct permits to drive. It sounds obvious, but you would be surprised how often these fundamentals are lacking.
- Get drivers into the habit of not starting the vehicle until everyone is wearing a seat belt.
- Insist that all speed limits are adhered to. If conditions are poor, consider implementing your own limits and inform the drivers they are not to exceed them. Never be afraid of asking a driver to slow down, especially if you are paying them.
- Make sure drivers understand the need to keep a safe distance from other vehicles, and enforce this. Two vehicle lengths is standard.
- Ensure that drivers do not use their mobile phones while driving. This is not negotiable.
- Although it might sound obvious, it is worth reiterating that drivers must not overtake on bends, on blind hills or anywhere where they cannot see that the road ahead is clear. In some countries, overtaking can happen at any time and in any place.
- Make sure, especially when driving in convoy, that drivers have (dipped) headlights on, even where possible during the day, so that their vehicles are more visible to oncoming traffic. Please note, however, that in some countries driving with lights on during the day is illegal, so do your research in advance.
- Insist that drivers take a break every two hours. This will keep them fresh and allow them, for example, to make any necessary phone calls.
- Look after your drivers: your life is in their hands, so make a point of making them feel valued.

WHAT TO DO IF IT ALL GOES WRONG

Be aware that if you are ever involved in, or witness an accident overseas, stopping to render assistance could be the worst thing you could do – and possibly the last thing. There are many accounts of well-intentioned travellers stopping to 'do the right thing', only to find themselves being robbed, beaten or killed. Equally, if you are responsible for accidentally injuring or killing someone, local justice can be swift and brutal. Don't put yourself in harm's way if you really don't have to: you will just be asking for trouble. Often the best and safest course of action is to drive on to the nearest police station and report the incident there. Ask for an interpreter if you don't understand what's being said, and make sure you get a copy of the police report.

If at all possible, make notes about what has happened and get photos of the accident, including pictures of the number plates of any other vehicles involved. Take the names and addresses of any witnesses, just as you would at home. All of this will be useful later on if you have to give evidence or make an insurance claim.

If you are driving the vehicle involved in the accident, be sure to inform your insurers, even if you don't want to make a claim. Insurance companies impose a time limit on the reporting of accidents, and if you fail to meet this you won't be covered if someone subsequently makes a claim against you.

If the vehicle is hired, contact the hire company as soon as possible, even if the accident was only minor. Give the company as much information about the accident as you can and never give the go-ahead on repairs without first getting their authorisation.

If you are injured in an accident, your insurance company should be able to help with finding appropriate medical care and getting you repatriated if required. Also contact your local consulate, which will be able to offer practical advice and support.

Laws vary from country to country, so the course of action that needs to be taken by the person responsible for the accident and by the victims will differ depending upon the location. Seek professional advice before taking any legal action.

VEHICLE SAFETY CHECKLIST

- The safest place to sit on a bus is in the middle of the vehicle. Passengers in the popular front seats often don't survive head-on collisions. Equally, if you are sitting at the back and it gets rear-ended you are more likely to be injured. Moreover, an aisle seat offers more protection from flying glass than a window seat, and for obvious reasons it's best to sit on the side of the bus furthest from oncoming traffic.
- Avoid travelling by road at night: you significantly increase your chances of an accident by travelling after dark. In developing countries, road lighting is often non-existent and often vehicles either don't have working lights or don't use them. There is also an increased risk of collisions with pedestrians, cyclists and animals.
- Check that the transport company you intend to use has a good reputation. What do online reviews say about them? Also, check whether the vehicle they propose using is suited to the conditions of the route you will be travelling. If not, you have to question how much emphasis they are actually placing on safety.
- Check whether the seats have proper seat belts. If yours does not, find another seat – or better still another vehicle. You can now take your own seat belt thanks to a company in the US called Safe Harness (see page 159).
- Does the vehicle have straps to secure any internal luggage? Insecure luggage flying at speed through the inside of a vehicle will do a lot of damage.
- Check whether the vehicle has an escape hammer for breaking the windscreen and the necessary tools for cutting through seat belts. Buses should have these fitted as standard, so make sure you know where they are and how to use them.

- Does the vehicle have a fire extinguisher?
- Check whether there is a tow rope with fixed hooks or a shackle. It could well get you out of a number of sticky situations. Similarly, is there a jack for changing tyres?
- Carry your own first aid kit (see page 155) and have it to hand, not stowed away in the luggage compartment. A torch will also be invaluable if there is an accident at night.
- If travelling in a car, avoid putting your luggage in the boot (trunk). There are far too many accounts of people having their belongings stolen from the boot of the vehicle they are travelling in whilst stuck in traffic. Try to keep personal belongings close to you and lock all the doors.
- If alone in a taxi always sit directly behind the driver and never in the front seat. If their intentions are not bona fide, sitting directly behind them makes you less accessible and provides a better chance of fleeing if you need to.
- If the vehicle breaks down, get it to the side of the road if possible, and make sure you get out and stay a safe distance away from it, encouraging others to do the same. Many stationary vehicles have been ploughed into whilst waiting for assistance to arrive. If you have an emergency warning triangle, use it. If not, use anything available to alert other road users – tree branches, rocks... anything that will alert other vehicles to the fact that you have broken down and are stationery. It's advisable to place warning signs at distances of 10 feet (3m), 100 feet (30m) and 200 feet (60m) from your vehicle so that they're visible to approaching traffic.
- Although it might sound like a lot of fun, motorcycles can be very dangerous, especially if you are unfamiliar with the driving standards and road conditions of the country you're in. Always wear a helmet and make sure you check your insurance policy, as many insurers don't cover the use of motorcycles and some expressly have it as an exclusion to the policy. Therefore, if you have an accident, you won't be covered for any medical or repatriation expenses and this could prove to be very costly.

CHAPTER EIGHT

BOAT SAFETY

Most travellers will probably have fantasised about sailing off to an idyllic tropical island or even chartering a boat for a spot of island hopping in the South Pacific. The prospect of any type of boating is certainly an enticing one but, as with all aspects of adventure travel, it's an activity that should be regarded with a note of caution.

Globally, death by drowning is more common than most people realise, and in certain areas of the world there are real dangers from piracy. To put this into perspective, it's worth looking at a few facts:

- According to the World Health Organization, drowning is the third leading cause of unintentional death worldwide, accounting for 7 per cent of all injury-related deaths.
- Every hour of every day more than 40 people lose their lives from drowning: nearly 400,000 drowning deaths are reported worldwide every year. However, there is considerable uncertainty around the actual number. Because of the way data is classified, the problem is much greater than the above figures reveal as they exclude intentional drowning deaths (suicide or homicide) and drowning deaths caused by flood disasters and water transport incidents.
- Every year there are 250–300 pirate attacks against ships worldwide.

While it is recognised that death by drowning and piracy are both global issues, there are also some significant regional risk variations that shouldn't be ignored:

- Low- and middle-income countries account for 96 per cent of unintentional drowning deaths.
- Drowning mortality rates are highest in Africa, where they are more than eight times higher than in Australia and the United States.
- China and India have particularly high drowning mortality rates and together contribute 43 per cent of the world's drowning deaths.
- Piracy is a particular problem in certain areas, including the Indian Ocean (especially off the coast of the Horn of Africa), coastal and river areas off some South American countries, the Malacca Straits, the South China Sea and the Red Sea.

But with a bit of forward planning and a few precautions, it is unlikely you will find yourself in harm's way.

MY STORY

I returned from Southeast Asia in 2001 and headed back to Africa. This time I was going to the west of the continent to recce a forthcoming expedition through Gambia and Senegal. I had been given a rather meagre budget for the trip so had to rely a great deal on local transport. Most of it was fine, but some was a little dodgy to say the least.

On one particular leg of the journey, I needed to cross the Gambia River from the capital, Banjul, to the town of Barra on the opposite bank. The Gambia River is wide and fast flowing and the public ferry was the only viable option. Another traveller had previously warned me that under no circumstances should I go below decks into the 'lounge' area of the ferry but that I should stay on top.

'The ferry is always overcrowded,' he said. 'It's unbearably hot below.'

I was determined to be one of the first on board so that I could ensure I had a decent position. I arrived early at the port and waited for the authorities to give permission to board. Large crowds swiftly gathered behind me, and I was pleased to be at the front of the queue.

When we were finally allowed to board, I looked around the upper deck for the best place to settle down for the short crossing. I located a locker that contained life jackets and sat down on it. I reasoned that, if the ferry did get into difficulties and go down, I would at least be able to grab a life jacket and get overboard quickly.

As I waited for the other passengers and vehicles to board, I couldn't help but notice that the large vessel was sinking lower and lower with each passing minute. The stream of foot passengers and vehicles seemed endless, and I began to feel very uneasy about how close the lower deck was getting to the water. Just when I thought it couldn't get any lower, the crew would load on another truck or car, accompanied by much shouting and hand waving.

I was beginning to seriously weigh up the possibility of getting off and abandoning the crossing when the crew drew up the ramp and threw off the ropes that attached us to the quay. With creaks and groans, the severely overloaded ferry started to make its slow laborious passage across the river.

I looked nervously around at my fellow passengers but none of the locals seemed the least bit worried. I, however, was feeling very uncomfortable indeed: I was convinced that we were continuing to sink lower and lower. The more I stared at it, the higher the river seemed to lap up the sides of the ferry. My only comfort was my ready access to the life jacket locker. I would at least stand a chance if we ended up sinking: as for just about everyone else, they were most likely doomed.

I was relieved when we eventually reached the other side and I vowed never again to take that ferry or any vessel like it.

A few years later, when I was back in the UK, I heard that a ship in Gambia had indeed sunk due to overcrowding. When I investigated the incident further, I was rather alarmed to learn that all the passengers who had been wearing life jackets had, in fact, drowned. This was not because the jackets were faulty but because passengers without life jackets regarded those who wore them as buoyancy aids. In their desperation to survive, they clung to them and, in doing so, forced those with life jackets under water.

IMPROVING THE ODDS

Any vessel you intend to travel on should have all the correct safety certificates and should comply with international maritime safety standards. Make sure that you check that the vessel has personal flotation devices (PFDs) on board and that you know where they are and how to access them. If they are stored below deck under a pile of other equipment, they are not going to be readily available in an emergency. This kind of chaotic management will also alert you to the vessel operator's lack of attention to safety issues.

Similarly, be sure to find out where the fire-fighting equipment is kept: the crew will usually be responsible for dealing with any fires but you may need to assist. And if you are not carrying your own, find out where the first aid kit is stored too.

You'll also need to locate the lifeboats or life rafts and make sure that they are SOLAS (Safety of Life at Sea) compliant; often they will be stamped accordingly. Also take note of how many passengers each lifeboat or raft is designed to take and then estimate the number of passengers on the vessel. If the passengers outnumber the lifeboat capacity, the vessel's operators are breaking international maritime law and you're on the wrong boat.

Don't be afraid to ask the captain or crew for any help with locating or checking any of these items: they should be more than willing to reassure you. They should also provide a full safety briefing before you depart. If you don't receive one, you have to ask whether they actually know what to do in an emergency. The briefing should include guidance on what to do in a man-overboard or abandon-ship situation and a guide to the location of the muster points.

All vessels should have at least one form of communication device: make sure you know where it is and that it's working. All passenger and cargo ships undertaking international voyages must have satellite communications, radio equipment, emergency position indicating radio beacons (EPIRBs) and search and rescue transponders (SARTs). In addition, vessels should carry a throw line or ring, safety lights, flares, a sound-producing device (such as a foghorn), paddles or oars and bailing equipment.

Don't ignore the weather conditions. In some countries, due to economic pressures and/or unscrupulous operators, crew may have no option but to set sail; you, however, always have the choice as to whether you get on the boat in the first place. You may not be an expert, but if it looks too rough from the safety of the shore, I guarantee it will be a lot worse when you are out there on the water. No voyage is that urgent that you should risk your life.

Ensure you have some protection from the elements. I have seen some very cold and wet people on boat journeys, as well as some very sunburnt ones. Sunblock and hats should be an essential part of your kit.

The Royal National Lifeboat Institution (RNLI) has some excellent information on their website about water safety, including dealing with riptides, cold water and tidal cut offs (see http://rnli.org/safety/respect-the-water). And before you go to sea, always check the sea-safety section of the relevant country's travel advice, particularly piracy reports if the area is prone to attacks.

WHAT TO DO IF IT ALL GOES WRONG

In the early hours of 23 November 2007, a small cruise ship called the MV Explorer struck ice in the Bransfield Strait off King George Island in Antarctica and started to sink. By 7:30 that morning all passengers and crew had abandoned ship and were in lifeboats awaiting rescue. I was on the incident management team that dealt with the situation, and while everyone survived, I have always remembered what was said to me by one of the passengers when I interviewed him after his repatriation to the UK.

I asked him whether there was any advice he would give to anyone who found themselves in a similar situation. He paused, thought long and hard, and then said, 'Yes. Never settle your bar bill until you reach your final port. Trust me, I've just saved myself a fortune.'

On a more serious note, generally speaking there are two main reasons why a ship will get into trouble: either it has taken on water or it has sprung a leak. Most incidents are due to the former, which tends to occur when a heavy storm strikes or a bilge pump malfunctions. The latter can be caused by a range of possibilities, including hitting floating debris, a fissure in the ship caused by a large wave, or missing equipment (such as a drain plug). If the vessel takes on more water than it can handle, it will eventually sink.

One of the most shocking aspects in either case is the speed of escalation. You need to be ready to react the moment you see things are going wrong.

Despite the warning at the end of my story, I would recommend that you slip on a life jacket immediately. If the worst happens and you do end up overboard, your odds of survival are far greater with a life jacket than without.

If something goes majorly wrong, your natural inclination will be to jump into the water and distance yourself from danger as quickly as possible. In most cases, though, the wisest course of action is, in fact, to stay on board a sinking ship as long as possible. Not only will you remain drier and warmer for longer but you will also present a larger target for rescuers to focus on.

Try to stay calm and listen to the captain's directions, which should include assigning jobs to crew and passengers, and directing them to gather flotation devices and prepare life rafts. Meanwhile, other crew members should be doing their best to resolve the source of the problem by blocking up leaks, bailing, operating pumps and so on. They should also by now have activated the EPIRB or SART and made a distress call via the emergency VHF radio, giving the boat's name and location, the number of people on board and any injuries so far reported.

As a large boat sinks, it will probably tilt, which can make it difficult to make your way around the deck. Hold on to the handrails and go slowly to prevent slipping, while keeping an eye out for large objects that may plough into you.

You'll know it's time to abandon ship when you hear a signal from the captain: seven short horn blasts followed by a long one. If it is safe to do so, make sure you take some supplies with you, such as your phone, an emergency radio, water, food and warm clothes, all packed in a waterproof bag.

If a mayday signal has gone out, rescue boats will be on their way. If you are on a smaller vessel which didn't manage to signal in time, your challenge is to make it to dry land, or at least to stay afloat until you are listed as overdue or are spotted by a passing boat or plane.

BOAT SAFETY CHECKLIST

- Always follow the crew's directions. Ship's crews are highly trained in rescue operations and should have an excellent understanding of what needs to be done to ensure everyone's safety. You should only 'do your own thing' if there is no proper authority to give you clear directions.

- If the captain assigns you a task and you don't feel up to the job, speak up immediately. Otherwise do your best to help out.

- Don't panic. This may sound like a cliché but you need to consciously stay calm. Studies have shown that 70 per cent of people suffer from impaired reasoning in an emergency like this, with 15 per cent becoming irrational. Just 15 per cent manage to keep their cool. Be aware that the opposite of panic – being so stunned that you are incapable of responding at all – can be just as much of a problem.

- If others around you are panicking, try to calm them down. If you see someone frozen with fear, shout at them. Flight attendants are trained to do this in emergencies to get people off planes.

- Concentrate on getting your breathing under control: this will help if you do end up in the water.

- If lifeboats are deployed, try to get into one without getting wet. If you do get wet you risk hypothermia or shock from the cold water. Cold-water shock occurs when water temperatures are at 15°C or below. It causes the blood vessels in the skin to close, which in turn raises the heart rate and increases blood pressure. This can lead to heart attacks even in the young and healthy.

- If you have to get off the ship and no lifeboats are available, look first where you're about to jump: there could be people, debris or propellers below you. Once in the water, watch out for floating objects, such as flotsam from the ship, which could help you stay afloat.

- Stay determined: stories of survival in water invariably show that those who remain resolute are the most likely to withstand the harsh conditions encountered before rescue.

CHAPTER NINE

ACCOMMODATION SAFETY

The last thing most people think about when travelling is whether the place where they're staying is secure. Having considered all the potential risks, from aircraft safety through to threats from kidnap through to natural disasters, there's a tendency to assume that accommodation can be left in the hands of hotel security. Wrong!

While many major hotels do have extensive security measures in place, the safety and security of your possessions is largely down to you. If you don't want to get back from an amazing day of exploration to discover your room has been burgled, it's in your interests to take a few precautions to protect yourself, at least against the most common threats.

The greatest risk is that your room will be broken into and your precious possessions stolen, including passports, credit cards and electronic equipment. Not only will this put a huge dampener on your whole trip but it will also mean that, to arrange replacements, you'll have to spend an enormous amount of time talking to the various organisations involved, including the hotel, the police and your insurance company.

Less commonly, you may find yourself the victim of a physical assault, perhaps as a prelude to burglary or theft, and there are obviously implications here for women travelling alone.

In addition, there could be a risk of fire in your accommodation, so you need to be fully aware of escape routes and how to respond in the event of an emergency.

Don't fool yourself into thinking that the majority of such incidents occur in developing countries: they are also common in major cities in countries all over the world.

Your accommodation should be your safe haven, particularly if you are travelling solo. This means choosing your room carefully and then taking precautions to keep it safe.

A FEW WORDS ON HOSTELS

Ava, a family friend of mine, is 18 years old and just starting out on what I'm sure will be a lifetime of travel and adventure. She and her cousin, Francesca, who is also 18, recently went travelling across Europe. It was their first real independent travelling adventure without their parents and both girls were excited. In fact, I was also pretty excited, as it brought back memories of the first time I set off to 'discover' the world. Before they embarked on their journey I went to see Ava and gave her a thorough safety briefing and also provided her with some essential travel safety kit. We went through just about every conceivable scenario, from what she and Francesca should do to avoid danger in the first place, to how they would need to react if they were confronted with a dangerous situation. By the end of the briefing day, everybody (especially Ava's parents) was happy that we had covered everything she needed for her forthcoming trip.

Their plan was to fly to Croatia and then inter-rail back to the UK, staying in local hostels along the way. By the time they reached Prague, they were becoming pretty savvy about travel safety and had employed many of the techniques we had discussed. The hostel they stayed in whilst in Prague resembled more of a classroom, or community hall than a traditional hostel. There was a large floor space with mattresses laid out where people could sleep and a shared basin in the corner of the room. Very basic, but they were only paying £10 (US$13) a night.

At about 10pm Ava and Francesca settled down on their mattresses and went to sleep, thankful that they were the only guests in the hostel that night. However, at midnight things changed. The lights went on and additional guests arrived at the hostel. But these guests weren't 18 year olds like Ava and Francesca. This was a group of 8 middle-aged men, who were loud, aggressive and very drunk.

The danger here was obvious and Ava and Francesca were clearly on edge, but they stayed calm, kept their personal alarms in one hand and their tactical flashlights in the other and remained poised to react. The drunken men eventually quietened down and slept off their booze-fuelled night, whilst Ava and Francesca rose early the next morning and left the hostel.

Whilst nothing untoward took place, this event highlights some of the vulnerabilities faced by travellers staying in shared accommodation. Therefore, it's vital that if you are staying in this type of accommodation, you increase your vigilance and personal security procedures.

Ava and Francesca returned home safely with plenty more tales of adventure, but certainly wiser about some of the dangers of travel.

It should be recognised that safety for female travellers is a subject all of its own and one that deserves specialist attention. Anyone travelling alone, whether on business or on holiday, should seriously consider taking a Sexual Assault Awareness & Prevention course. These courses are run by experts, including former and serving police officers, and cover how to avoid dangerous situations and what to do if you are confronted or assaulted. They include sessions on many of the subjects covered in this book, as well as gender-specific topics such as understanding legal and cultural differences and how to defuse a conflict situation.

MY STORY

After surviving the ferry crossing of the Gambia River (see pages 110–112), the next leg of my African journey was by bus. I had to stow my rucksack on the roof, which is pretty standard when travelling in poorer parts of the world. Experience has taught me to lock everything securely, and I was pleased to see that there was a purpose-made lockable wire cage in which my rucksack could be stored.

When I got to my destination, however, I discovered that someone – probably a member of the numerous bus crew – had managed to open the side pockets and remove the contents. Given the time it would have taken to painstakingly ease his way through the wire mesh, the robber was no doubt rather disappointed: the side pockets were where I kept my dirty underwear and socks.

When we reached the town of Toubakouta, I hired a car and driver for the journey to the Senegalese capital, Dakar. Although I gave the driver all the usual safety briefings and instructions on how I wanted him to drive, we still ran into trouble.

We were about 60 miles from our destination when we saw a shepherd herding his goats by the roadside. It was a fair-sized herd and I asked my driver to slow down, as I didn't want him to hit any of the goats. He paid no attention but, if anything, sped up while aggressively honking his horn. It was inevitable that we were going to hit a goat and sure enough that's exactly what we did.

Unfortunately for the goat, the car didn't kill it outright. In fact, what it did was to break its back, which left its hind legs useless as it struggled to get back on to its front legs. It was a distressing sight although the animal looked more confused than in pain.

The car came to a halt and I urged my driver to go back

and finish the poor thing off. He refused point-blank: the shepherd would be looking for revenge and payment for the goat, he said. Sure enough, just as we began to drive away, the shepherd appeared on the scene. I saw him produce a large knife from beneath his clothing. The menacing way in which he brandished it made me decide that this was clearly not the time for negotiation.

My driver was now very nervous but I ordered him to stop the car. I took the keys from the ignition as I got out so he couldn't drive off and leave me stranded with the angry shepherd. I took some money from my wallet, about the equivalent of US$20, and held it up in clear sight so that the shepherd, who was about 30 yards away from us, could see what it was. I pointed at the dying goat and placed the money under a rock at the side of the road. I then got back in the car and gave the keys to the driver, and we drove off.

As I looked back, I saw the shepherd putting the goat out of its misery and then walking over to the rock. I was livid with the driver and didn't hold back in telling him so.

When I eventually got to Dakar, I paid the driver the amount we had agreed back in Toubakouta but he still had the cheek to ask for a tip. I told him that I'd given his tip to the shepherd. He wasn't best pleased but perhaps it would teach him to drive more carefully in future.

I had been really looking forward to reaching Dakar as a friend of mine had given me a voucher for a five-star hotel in the city. The hotel was part of a well-known international chain and would be a welcome break from the somewhat basic local accommodation I had frequented since arriving in West Africa.

I'm sure I appeared out of place as I entered the hotel reception in my filthy travelling clothes, in desperate need of a wash. The other guests I saw were French tourists, looking tremendously chic in the latest Paris fashions.

I checked in and went straight to my room for a long shower before sorting my clothes for the laundry service. I was urgently in need of clean socks and underwear given that half of mine had been stolen.

The hotel was a world away from what I had been used to. It had a luxurious swimming pool and even its own golf course. I made the most of the amenities, since the next day I would be back on public transport for the long journey to St Louis.

When the evening came, I sat in the bar and had a few beers before devouring a sumptuous meal, the price of which was also included in the voucher. I drank a toast to my friend for his generosity and returned to my room to pack and get some sleep. The bed was huge and the bedding was so soft that I dropped off almost immediately.

At about 3am I suddenly awoke to find that I was no longer alone. I don't know what woke me but I was fully alert. I saw two figures creeping towards my bag, which was at the far side of the room near the window.

I shouted loudly at them. I can't remember the exact words I used but the language was colourful. Immediately they darted back towards the door. I jumped out of bed and gave chase. (I always wear something in bed, incidentally: you never know when you might have to leave your room in a hurry.)

The first intruder got to the door and pelted off down the corridor. The second wasn't so fast and I caught him just as he was leaving the room.

With all the commotion it wasn't long before other residents, awoken from their slumbers, were venturing into the corridor to see what was going on. I asked them, in my best French, to call security, which someone duly did. Within moments, a couple of overweight, out-of-shape men in ill-fitting uniforms appeared, along with the duty manager, who fortunately spoke English.

I explained what had happened and his response caught me by surprise.

'But sir, this man is one of our staff!' he said, looking dumbfounded.

'Well, why wasn't he wearing his uniform and what the hell was he doing in my room at 3am?' I replied, feeling quite angry now.

The manager put the question to the intruder, who insisted that he was only coming in to put chocolates on my pillows. Now it was my turn to be dumbfounded.

'At 3 o'clock in the morning?' I said. 'Where are the chocolates then?'

That question completely threw the would-be robber, who managed to stutter out that his friend had them. The moment the words came out of his mouth, his face fell. He suddenly realised he had just dropped his mate in it. His story was unravelling by the second.

The manager told me that he would conduct a full investigation and that he would have a report for me in the morning. He urged me to go back to bed and said that he would deal with his staff.

Unsurprisingly, I couldn't get back to sleep so I read until 6am, when breakfast was served. After having something to eat, I went to find the night manager, only to learn that he had already finished his shift and gone home. There was no report.

I asked to see the new duty manager and quickly found that he knew nothing about the incident. He called for the head of security, who also seemed to know nothing.

By now it was becoming patently clear that this was an inside job and that the staff were closing ranks. Having worked in Africa before and knowing how the system operates, I decided that my only option was to call the hotel's headquarters in Paris.

It was only then that I started to see any meaningful action. I was asked to write a report and fax it through to them. After that my complaint was taken much more seriously, or so I was led to believe. But even so the hotel refused to get the police involved unless I insisted on pressing criminal charges against the two men who had entered my room.

They did offer to waive the cost of the room, but as I'd got it on a voucher anyway, that was no compensation. So I negotiated for one of their drivers to take me to St Louis in a hotel minibus, which was obviously preferable to public transport and by far the safer option.

The final insult came when I tried to check out and discovered that they had charged me for the phone call and fax to their Paris HQ. Naturally, I refused to pay.

On that occasion I was lucky. I woke up in the nick of time and managed to get the upper hand over the intruders. That said, I believe their intention was simply to rob and not to cause me harm. If I had been a single female alone in the room, however, the outcome could have been very different.

This story demonstrates the importance of maintaining vigilance with regards to your accommodation, no matter how exclusive it may be. Always deadlock your door and don't rely just on the electronic lock. These can be compromised by staff, as happened in this case, and since then I have always taken additional in-room security measures.

IMPROVING THE ODDS

When you're planning your trip, check to see whether the hotel you've chosen is located in a good part of town. The last thing you want is to end up in the centre of a high-crime area. Check out online reviews to read about the experiences of other travellers and learn how they rate the security risks.

When you first arrive at your hotel, be sure to keep your luggage with you at all times: don't rely on hotel staff to keep it safe. Many people have their luggage stolen when checking in or checking out of their hotel.

Keep your wits about you and watch out for people who are standing too close to you or who appear to be listening in on your conversations. They might be trying to find out which room you are in and whether you are travelling alone. If they see you later on in the restaurant or by the pool, they will know that your room is unoccupied.

For the same reason, if the receptionist announces your room number when handing you the key, don't accept it: everyone within earshot will know which room you're in. If the reception area is crowded, ask the receptionist to write the number down on a piece of paper or share it with you non-verbally in some other way.

Never accept a room on the ground floor, as these are the easiest for criminals from outside to break into. Rooms between the second and fourth floors are best, and you should be OK in the event of a fire, as most fire-department ladders reach up to the fourth storey.

If you are in a hostile environment where terrorism is a problem, avoid rooms overlooking a car park and in this case ask for a room on the fifth floor or above. The blast from a car bomb usually devastates the first four storeys.

Check that the hallways and grounds, including car parks, are well lit; if not, they are likely to attract criminals. I used to stay in a hotel in Boston that appeared fine during the day but whose car park turned into an open market for drug dealers the moment it got dark.

Elevators can be dangerous places, particularly for women on their own. If a suspicious-looking character gets in, leave the elevator as soon as possible. You can always claim you have forgotten something and go back down to the lobby.

Where possible, select a hotel that has installed electronic keycard locks. Old-fashioned metal keys are usually hung up behind the reception desk, so if a criminal wants to see who is in and who is out, they only have to look behind the desk.

If your hotel is still using metal keys, never leave the key in the door when you are in the room. Criminals have been known to slide a piece of paper under the door and then push the key out from the other side with a screwdriver. When the key drops on to the paper, they simply slide it back under the door and can then access your room with your key.

As soon as you check in to your room, test that the door lock and the deadlock are working. If they're not, ask for a new room. Whenever you are inside your hotel room, make sure you use the deadlock, and it's also worth investing in a device that jams the door. This can be a simple door wedge that is inserted on your side of the door, or something more elaborate, such as a door jammer.

Check that your room has a peep hole so that, if anyone knocks, you can see who's there. If you are unsure whether the person at the door is legitimate, call reception and ask them to confirm that your caller is genuine. Tell the caller what you're doing: if they are genuine they will understand; if not they are likely to leave before security arrives.

When you settle down for the night, make it difficult for anyone to get into your room. If the en-suite bathroom is situated near the entrance and the bathroom door opens outwards, consider opening it and putting a wedge under the door in addition to the one under the main door. An intruder won't be expecting a second barrier and certainly not a door wedged in position.

I often move hotel room furniture around in order to create additional barriers. At night I might move a table close to the door and place a lamp on the very edge of it. That way, if someone does get in, the ensuing clatter will hopefully deter them and wake me. Equally, with balcony doors, I always draw the curtains and place items of furniture and luggage in positions where would-be intruders will trip over them.

The best place for valuables is in a hotel safe, not in your bags. However, be aware that in-room safes can be compromised, even when you choose the combination. All such safes have a default, which means that dishonest hotel staff can open them. Whatever you do, don't swipe your credit card as the means by which you open the safe. Many people have had their card details stolen by these types of safe.

One of the first things you should do when you get to your room is to make sure you know where the nearest fire exit is. Count the doors from your room to the exit. If a fire breaks out, it may well be dark and the corridor may be full of smoke. I also like to walk the route to the fire exit and make sure that the fire exit doors are not locked. If they are, inform reception and ask for them to be unlocked.

Also check that the fire exits are not blocked from the outside. In a hotel in Argentina I once found a large wheelie bin blocking a fire exit. The staff weren't even aware it was there. On another occasion, in Estonia, I was told that the fire exit door was intentionally locked to keep non-guests out, but that in an emergency the receptionist would be available to unlock it. I checked out of there and found another hotel: I can pretty much guarantee that in an emergency such as a fire the receptionist will be too busy saving their own skin to unlock the fire exit door for the guests.

Pay attention to whether your room has a smoke detector and sprinkler and whether there is fire-fighting equipment in the corridor, such as a sprinkler system and fire extinguishers. In the event of a fire these could save your life.

WHAT TO DO IF IT ALL GOES WRONG

If your hotel room is burgled, contact the authorities immediately. Even if they can't get your things back for you, you will need a copy of the police report for insurance purposes. If your passport goes missing, you must contact your embassy immediately. Not only will you need to arrange a replacement but you will also need to report it stolen so that no one else can make use of it. Be sure to carry with you copies of important documents such as passport, flight itineraries, driver's licence and travel insurance: this will make things a whole lot easier in the event something does go wrong.

If your wallet or purse has been stolen, contact your bank and credit card company to report the theft. You don't want the thieves to go on a spending spree at your expense. Get in touch with your travel insurance provider, who will again require a copy of the police report.

If your hotel has an electronic door lock, you can ask for a reading from the system to see when the room was accessed and by whom. It may show whether the room was entered by someone who stole your keycard or by a robber who snuck in on the off chance while the room was being cleaned.

In the event of a fire, if it is safe to do so, leave your room immediately, keep low and crawl to the nearest fire exit. Do not use the elevator. If you are unable to escape from your room, fill the bath and the sink in your bathroom with water, leave the taps running and let them both overflow. Place wet towels under the door and over any vents. If it's safe to do so, open your curtains and wave bed sheets to attract the attention of the emergency services. They won't necessarily know which rooms are occupied, so help them (and yourself) out by alerting them to your presence.

ACCOMMODATION SAFETY CHECKLIST

- Read the small print of your hotel registration documents. They detail exactly what the hotel will or won't cover in terms of theft. Typically, hotels do not insure their guests' belongings.
- As a rule, leave the bling at home when travelling, taking as few valuable items as you can. Don't leave passports, tickets, technology or cameras lying around your room. Dispose of receipts carefully so that you don't leave yourself open to identity theft.
- Every time you leave the room take a moment to check that the door is locked.
- Making your room look as though it's occupied will go some way to deterring thieves. Simply leave the TV or radio on at a low

volume, and if your room doesn't need cleaning, hang a 'do not disturb' sign on the door. This also eliminates the possibility of someone pretending they are staying in your room and 'nipping in' to get something while the cleaner is working. The 'do not disturb' sign, however, is not a foolproof way of keeping cleaners out: you may need to contact the front desk and put in a specific request that your room should not be cleaned.

- It's always wise to have a small grab bag beside your bed in case you ever have to leave your room in a hurry. This should contain a torch, your phone, your passport, some cash and your room key. You should also have a pair of shoes next to your bed, as in a fire the floor could get very hot.
- If you are attacked in an elevator, press as many floor buttons as possible, as soon as possible.

CHAPTER TEN

TERRORISM

Terrorism can prove a very real threat to travellers. There have been numerous accounts of terrorists specifically targeting tourists to gain publicity for their cause, and incidences seem to have increased in scope, variety and intensity in recent years. However, this is not a new phenomenon. Whilst it may appear that terrorism is a very real threat to travellers these days, I would reiterate that your chances of getting caught in a terror attack are 1 in 20 million. Despite what the media would have us believe, these attacks are very rare, especially when compared with other travel hazards such as traffic related incidents. However, they do happen and attacks can take many forms, including suicide operations, hijackings, bombings, kidnappings, shootings and attacks on commercial aircraft and ships.

In 1997, 62 people – 58 of them foreign tourists – were massacred in Luxor, Egypt. A year later, three British nationals and an Australian were kidnapped and killed while on an adventure holiday in Yemen. In 2015, 38 tourists were killed while holidaying in Sousse, Tunisia, just months after an attack at the Bardo National Museum in Tunis which had led to the deaths of 22 people, including 20 foreigners. Then there have been the attacks in Paris in November 2015, as well as subsequent attacks in Berlin, Nice, Stockholm, and more recently in London, Manchester and Barcelona... These events may not be the norm but they certainly do happen.

The one thing they all have in common is that they targeted ordinary people going about their everyday business. Sousse and the attack on the Russian Metro-Jet aircraft departing Sharm el Sheikh specifically targeted tourists, while Paris, London, Manchester and Barcelona focused on people enjoying normal social activities, such as strolling, having a coffee with friends or going to a concert. All these attacks took place in areas frequented by tourists which would have previously been regarded as 'safe'.

Recent attacks have also seen the rise of vehicles being used as weapons in order to cause massive destruction, injury and, sadly, death. This type of attack has highlighted the need for greater public vigilance. Not only do attacks need to be prevented in the first place, but we also need to understand how to react once an attack is underway. A key part of this is, again, situational awareness. It's an effective tool for those trained how to use it properly.

However, situational awareness requires an understanding of what is normal, so that a baseline can be established and anomalies can be identified. In the London, Nice, Berlin and Barcelona attacks, vehicles were used as weapons. People expect to see vehicles on our streets, so how do we tell the difference between those going about their normal business and those with malicious intent? After all, those who would do us harm rely on the fact that they are able to blend in to carry out their attacks. Therefore, it's the small pre-event indicators we need to be aware of – the change in engine pitch, the screech of tyres or the sound of people shouting.

Unfortunately, most people are not attuned to such warning signs. Not only are most people not trained, but many also wander around in their own world, sometimes with headphones on or concentrating on their smartphones. This in turn deprives them of the vital senses that could make the difference between being able to react to a situation and becoming a victim.

Sadly, there are times when even with the best situational

awareness and personal security procedures in place, the speed of events leaves little or no time to react.

Many of the eyewitnesses of the attack in Tunisia said that when they first heard the shooting they thought of fire crackers. Unfortunately, we no longer live in a world where we can associate loud bangs with fireworks and celebrations. We should be thinking of bombs, bullets and evasive action.

Many people have been left wondering whether there is anywhere at all that is still safe. It is worth noting that the Foreign & Commonwealth Office rates the threat of terrorism in the UK as 'high', as is also the case in Australia, France and Spain. In other words, it can be just as dangerous to stay at home, particularly if you're in one of the major cities. For those looking further afield, the FCO website lists a number of regions where 'essential travel only' is recommended, as well as other areas that should be avoided altogether. In some countries, where there have already been attacks, the advice is simply to practise increased vigilance. It's certainly worth visiting the 'know before you go' section of the FCO website as part of your travel planning.

There are some great free Open Source Intelligence (OSINT) resources available online. These allow people to make an informed decision as to whether or not their risk appetite allows them to travel to a particular country or region.

I would also encourage travellers to look at other nations' equivalents of the Foreign Office. The Australian Smart Traveller website is exceptionally good and in many cases goes into a lot more detail than the FCO does.

There's also something called OSAC (Overseas Security Advisory Council), which is a US government site for US government personnel working overseas. They have various reports and warnings that will go out for different countries if there is a safety issue.

Using the FCO, Smart Traveller or OSAC sites would give you a pretty good overview to make an informed decision on your travel choices.

It must be said, however, that hundreds of thousands of tourists visit and enjoy many of these 'higher-risk' countries every year, in the vast majority of cases completely trouble-free (barring the odd pickpocket or two). Tourism forms a vital financial lifeline for the economies of many countries, and many travel destinations have taken strong measures to protect visitors.

Whether you choose to travel to higher-risk destinations is your personal decision, but if you do, the basic advice is to remain vigilant and follow the instructions of local authorities.

MY STORY

I was in Herefordshire on a long and intensive training programme in how to survive hostile environments. I had attended the course in order to update and refresh my skills, which is something I never compromise on. The right kind of training is crucial preparation when you're about to enter a difficult or dangerous foreign environment. The course was run by former British special forces personnel and was designed specifically for those working in the world's trouble hotspots. Most of the attendees were either journalists or security operatives. In the final part of the course we were placed in a scenario, made to appear as realistic as possible, which was critical in enabling participants to get some idea of what can actually happen in some of the more volatile regions of the world. My role was working for a company called Intrepid TV and our brief was to travel to a remote area of Yemen that had, until recently, been held by Al-Qaeda. We had been given permission to visit the site by the Yemeni military; we had also been given assurances by both the military and our fixer that the route to the site and the site itself were secure.

Our preparation had been meticulous. We'd done everything we'd been trained to do to ensure the safety of the team.

Our driver was a trusted local man who had recently taken international teams of journalists to Jaar, and we had researched alternative routes in and out of the city in case ours became compromised. The vehicle itself was deliberately inconspicuous and I had checked it over very carefully before deeming it fit for the task.

There were five of us due to travel in the vehicle: the driver, two journalists, a cameraman and myself, acting as security. The drive would take about an hour and a half, and then it would be a further 20 minutes to the site of the mass grave.

I got into the front beside the driver and the rest of the team piled in the back. I gave a final briefing before we set off in order to recap our security procedures, with which by now everyone was very familiar. I did a final check to ensure that we all had our press passes to hand and we headed off.

The journey was pretty unremarkable, and we spent a lot of the time listening to our driver tell us stories about his 12 children. Once we left the main highway, though, the mood changed and there was a notable tension in the air.

I said to the driver, 'How much further to the site?'

He smiled at me reassuringly and replied, 'Not far now, Mr Lloyd. Maybe five more minutes.'

We were driving down a tree-lined track and it was difficult to see what was ahead.

The first I knew that something was wrong was when I saw hooded gunmen appear in the road. They were pointing their AK-47s directly at us and shouting in Arabic. Even without the benefit of knowing the language it was very clear they wanted us to stop. Instinctively we all raised our hands while simultaneously trying to show our press passes.

'Journalists, journalists!' we shouted as they opened the doors and dragged us out of the car.

It was then that I spotted another team of journalists who had left in another vehicle just ahead of us. They were lying face down on the ground with black hoods over their heads and their hands tied behind their backs.

Instantly, my drills kicked in and I did a quick head count. I reckoned that there were seven gunmen in the group and they were highly agitated. I could see the five journalists from the other group, but not their driver.

Our own driver was then separated from us and taken behind our vehicle. Suddenly, a single shot rang out. That would explain what had happened to the other driver. These people were not in the mood to mess about. I was surprised at how well organised they seemed to be.

I was marched to the side of the track with the muzzle of an AK-47 in my back and told to kneel down. A hood was placed over my head and I was kicked to the ground, landing on my face. Another boot went into my ribs for good measure. I could feel someone going through my pockets and removing my phone, wallet, notebook and a map I had of the area. I was still holding my press pass but that was soon snatched from my fingers. Things were happening very fast.

I was given a few more kicks and I felt a pistol thrust against the base of my skull. I was conscious of just how hot it was inside the hood.

'On your feet,' a voice ordered.

As soon as I'd scrambled up, I was marched down the track a short distance and made to kneel.

'What's your name?' the voice demanded. He spoke good English: I guessed he was in charge.

'Lloyd.'

'What are you doing here?' he barked.

'I'm a journalist with Intrepid TV. We're covering the situation in Yemen.'

'Hold this,' the man ordered. Something bulky was thrust into my right hand. 'You are not a journalist,' he continued. 'You are a spy and you mean to harm Islam. Where are you from?'

My training told me that I must at all costs remain calm and not rise to his accusations.

'My name is Lloyd, I am a journalist for Intrepid TV and I am from the UK.'

I heard him tell the person holding the gun to my head to remove my hood. I blinked at the sudden influx of light.

'If you are not a spy and you don't mean harm to Islam, why did we find this thing you are holding in your car?'

I looked down and saw that I was holding a crude bomb made of C4 explosive with a timer attached. I also saw that there was a video camera right in front of me and an armed guard at each side. I caught a glimpse of an Al-Qaeda flag, just behind me. The man asking the questions had his face covered but his eyes were filled with anger.

'I am not a spy and I don't know where this came from,' I said firmly, with the lightest of nods at the 'bomb'. 'It was not in our car. My name is Lloyd and I am a journalist with Intrepid TV. I mean no harm to you or to Islam.'

I could feel his eyes burning into me but I didn't look directly at him in case he saw it as a sign of arrogance or aggression.

'Look into the camera and tell me your name, where you are from and that you are a spy,' he said, his voice hardening further.

'My name is Lloyd. I am a journalist from the UK.'

He lent forward and pressed his pistol to my forehead.

'You are a spy. You are not a journalist. You are the security man. The others have already told me so. Now tell the camera.'

He was getting agitated and I knew that if I admitted I was a spy I was as good as dead. Conceding that I was part of the security detail would most likely have had the same outcome: it's customary to get rid of security operatives pretty quickly, in order to neutralise any threat they may pose.

'My name is Lloyd. I'm a journalist.'

This time the man didn't respond. Instead, he turned and walked away to my right, where a man was lying on the ground, face down and hooded. He gave him a sharp kick.

'What's your name and where are you from?'

The man on the ground replied, 'My name is Jack. I'm a journalist from the UK.'

Jack and I had arrived together. He was a young freelancer and I liked him. A shot rang out and a puff of dust rose up next to Jack.

'Tell me you're a spy or the next one goes in his head,' the man demanded, looking straight at me.

I looked directly into the camera lens and said, 'My name is Lloyd Figgins and I'm a spy.'

As the words fell from my mouth, I felt utterly defeated.

The masked man played back the recording to make sure he had what he wanted and then told one of the guards to replace my hood. Everything went dark again.

I was forced back to my feet and marched further along the path, away from the rest of the group, with an AK-47 planted firmly in the small of my back.

'On your knees, infidel,' barked a guard. I was pushed into a kneeling position. I guessed that whatever came next was not going to be good.

I heard the voice of the man who had taken the video footage calmly say, 'You are a security operative and we don't have any use for you, so now you will be executed.'

I felt his pistol pressing into the back of my neck and thought, *So this is how it ends*. The next sound I heard was a shot ring out close to my ear, followed by a wild laugh from my tormentor.

'Next time, spy. Next time.'

I knelt there, frozen to the spot, my hands still in the air. I was well aware that the mock execution is a way to spread fear among us all and assert control.

I could hear others from our group being dragged in front of the camera and ordered to read a statement that said they were infidels and enemies of Islam. They were humiliating us, one by one, but it didn't escape my notice that I was the only one accused of spying. I was also the only one to be separated out from the rest.

A few minutes later, I heard a loud scream from one of the female journalists. Within moments she was pushed to the floor beside me.

We knelt next to one another for what seemed like an eternity before she broke the silence.

'Are you OK, Lloyd?' she whispered. It was Jo. She and I had been in the same vehicle and she had seen me getting a bit of a kicking.

'I'm fine,' I whispered back.

There was a pause before she said, 'I'm not wearing a hood.'

This was critical information.

'Tell me what you can see,' I whispered.

Speaking softly, Jo explained that there was a path in front of us. She couldn't see where it went but there were no obvious guards. Behind us, the commotion of the video 'interviews' was still carrying on.

I suspected that we were not being watched that closely, so I slowly started to lower my arms. I knew that, if someone was guarding us, I would be told to get my hands back up, and that this would probably be accompanied with a kick or a painful blow from a rifle butt.

Feeling slightly more confident, I shuffled in my position. If someone was watching me they were bound to say something.

I said quietly, 'Jo, we have to get out of here. If we stay, they are going to kill us.'

Her response betrayed the fear she must have been feeling.

'I don't think I can. I'm too scared.'

I was also afraid, but I knew that if we stayed where we were, we were almost certainly out of the game.

'I'm going to count to three, and then we're both going to run straight ahead as fast as we can. You can't look back and you can't stop. No matter what happens or what you hear, you have to keep going. Do you understand me?'

Jo didn't respond. I knew that the longer I gave her to think about it, the more the doubts would creep into her mind.

'One, two, three...'

I whisked off my hood, to see Jo take off like a greyhound out of the traps. I leapt to my feet and ran full-pelt after her.

We ran for some considerable distance without stopping. I was determined to get off the path and put as much ground as possible between us and our attackers. There were likely to be other 'unfriendlies' in the area, and we would be easy to find along the track.

After a time, I grabbed hold of Jo and dragged her into the undergrowth.

'We have to stay off the paths, Jo,' I said, panting.

My heart was thumping against my chest and I could see that Jo was in a similar state of exhaustion. We stayed still for a few minutes before I was convinced we weren't being followed.

'Jo, we have to move and head back towards safety.'

'I can't move,' she gasped. She seemed to be paralysed by fear. 'You go. You have a better chance of making it without me.'

They would be searching for us soon, and the longer we left it, the more chance we had of getting caught. Jo didn't look capable of going anywhere so I told her to stay exactly where she was and not move an inch, no matter what happened or what she heard. I covered her up with some vegetation and made sure she couldn't be seen from the path, and then I set off. I hated to leave her but I knew that if I got to safety I could go back for her with the cavalry.

I was running down a hill and hadn't got far before I came across a small overhang to the side covered by vegetation. I carefully scaled down over the overhang and found a good hiding place against the cliff wall. I stopped there for a while to assess the situation.

I could hear traffic in the far distance, and a busy road seemed like the best place for finding help. The challenge was that the terrain between my current position and the road was densely vegetated, and our attackers could be anywhere. I would have to be extra-vigilant and move only when I was absolutely certain it was safe to do so. Ideally, I would wait for nightfall, but that would greatly reduce the chances of Jo and the rest of the group getting out.

My thoughts were interrupted by voices directly above me. I couldn't make out what they were saying or even what language they were speaking, but it sounded like there were no more than two of them. If my original head count had been correct, there were only seven gunmen in all, so they couldn't afford to spread themselves too thinly or they risked losing more prisoners. The fact there had been no obvious commotion suggested that they still hadn't found Jo.

As they got closer to the cliff edge, I heard their footsteps just above me. After a few minutes they moved away and I could breathe again. Something told me that they wouldn't find me now unless I was careless. I lay down, made myself comfortable and, for the first time since the abduction, relaxed a little.

I couldn't relax for long: I heard voices again, this time below me. It was probably the same people extending their search area. From my elevated position, there was little point in taking a peek over the cliff, and moving would only increase my risks of being detected. I would just have to wait until they moved on.

Once I could no longer hear them, I risked a look over the cliff. There were no signs of people and no human-generated sounds. The birds, however, had started singing again, which was a sign that the searchers had probably moved on.

I estimated that I had a good couple of miles of no man's land to negotiate before I reached the road. And in an area like that anything could happen. It could be mined or booby-trapped, and I could, of course, run straight into the people who were searching for me. Regardless of the risks, though, I had no choice but to attempt to cross the terrain in order to get to safety.

The time for waiting was over and I moved as quickly and quietly as I could. My heart was pounding again and I was breathing heavily. As I got to the edge of the vegetation, I took cover again and re-assessed my options. There were at least two large fields between me and my goal and a path running between them. I opted to avoid this at all costs and plotted a circuitous route towards the road. Apart from the hedge that ran along one side of it, it would be pretty open.

I tried to calculate how much ground there was between the place where I'd last heard the search party and the first field. I figured it to be about 200 yards (180m). Provided they didn't have anything more powerful than AK-47s, I would need to get at least another 200 yards away in order to be out of effective firing range. If I kept to the left side of the hedge and stayed low, I reckoned I could get out of range in under a minute, and then it would be an all-out dash to the road.

There was no point hanging around. I took a deep breath and jumped the small fence between the vegetated area and the field. I crouched down and ran for all I was worth, expecting to hear the crack of automatic weapon fire at any second. The gunfire never came, and with every step my confidence grew that I would get away.

As I got closer to the road, I became nervous again. I took cover and assessed my position. I could see a hotel I'd noticed earlier when we'd driven in, and it was no more than 500 yards away. Weighing up my options, I decided it would be safer to head there than to flag down a random car. The way my luck had gone today, I would probably wave down the bad guys. If I made it to the hotel, on the other hand, I should at least be on neutral ground and could then get together a rescue party in search of Jo and the others.

Crouched low behind the hedge, I waited for a gap in the traffic. When the coast was clear, I darted across the road and behind another hedge that ran parallel with it. Something told me not to go to the front entrance of the hotel, so I skirted around the back and went in via the garden at the rear. I could see the hotel staff going about their daily business, and there was no sign that anything untoward was going on.

I walked into the hotel, sweating heavily and covered in dirt. The first person I met was Jo. She glanced at me and said, 'I wondered how long it would take you to get here. You look a right state!'

Then one of the course instructors appeared.

'We thought you would go into escape-and-evasion mode, Figgins. Well done. You're the only one who made it back without being recaptured. Now get yourself cleaned up and get back to the classroom.'

The course had been perfectly timed. Two weeks later I was working in the Middle East where I was able to put into practice much of what I had learnt. At this stage, I was running fewer expeditions and doing more risk-management and security work. I'd been asked to do some work in Syria, and deployment to the Middle East in December 2001 was not an assignment I was going to take lightly. The 9/11 attacks in the United States had taken place a few months earlier and the west's reaction had affected the entire region. The actions of Al-Qaeda and its success against the USA had had the effect of uniting Islamic groups. Tensions were high, as were anti-western feelings.

I travelled from the capital, Damascus, to the ancient city of Palmyra. After just a short time there it became very apparent that there was a palpable tension in the air. The local people told me that Hezbollah and other groups were trying to take advantage of world events and gain influence in the area.

On my third evening in Palmyra, I went for dinner to a café

I'd already visited a couple of times before. The owner was the cousin of the man who owned the hotel I was staying in and he always treated me well. My previous visits had been problem-free, but on this occasion I was in trouble the second I walked through the door.

Two men were deep in conversation over in the far corner, and as soon as they saw me they stopped talking and called the owner over. They were clearly agitated and kept glaring at me. The owner then turned away from them and glanced over to me, looking as if he had seen a ghost.

These blokes were trouble. The lighting in the café was poor, but from my position at the table where I'd seated myself, I took as good a look at them as I could. I wanted to know what I was dealing with.

The elder of the two had an eye missing; he had made no attempt to cover the socket with a patch. The younger man looked particularly pent up. He had his back to me but kept swivelling round in his chair to eye me up and down.

They called the owner over again and the heated debate continued, this time at a much higher volume. Not being an Arabic speaker, I had no idea what they were saying, but it was definitely about me and undoubtedly far from positive.

Without warning the one-eyed man suddenly stood up and started shouting at the owner, making threatening gestures. Then he turned his attention to me. The words meant nothing but I could tell from the tone of his voice that his intentions were hostile. Next his mate stood up and he too started shouting at me. Now that he was standing I could see that this bloke was huge – at least six feet four (1.90m) and powerfully built.

The owner was doing his best to calm them down but without success. They were becoming increasingly hysterical and were clearly feeding off each other's anger.

I was totally bemused: I'd only nipped in for a kebab. I began looking at the nearest exit.

By now the owner was trying to usher the men out of the door while they continued to hurl abuse at me. Eventually they were out and into the night.

Then, inexplicably, he calmly turned to me, smiled and asked what I would like to order. The situation was truly bizarre.

'What was the problem?' I asked.

'No problem, you eat,' he said, with a dismissive wave of his hand.

I ordered my kebab along with some local bread, hummus and a salad, and I tried to put the events behind me. As I tucked into my supper, I heard a phone ring in the back of the restaurant and the owner went to the kitchen to answer it.

Within seconds he came darting out, ran outside and began to yank down the metal shutter on the outer side of the windows. When it was three-quarters of the way down he ducked back through the door and, from the inside, finished pulling the shutter all the way to the ground. He then closed the door firmly and locked it before turning to me, his only customer. His face was ashen.

'We must leave quickly,' he said.

I didn't argue. I got to my feet to follow him through to the kitchen.

'Quick, quick,' he kept urging.

I stuck as close to him as possible as we threaded our way through the chaotic and cramped cooking area. When we got to the other end, he opened the back door, which led out into an alley. He poked his head out and had a quick look up and down and then told me to follow him.

We couldn't have got more than 15 yards down the alley when I heard the first explosion. Another followed very shortly afterwards.

I wanted to look behind me but there was no time to waste so I just ran. The café owner led me through a labyrinth of dark alleys at a tremendous pace. I had no idea where we were.

It seemed we had been running for ages but in truth it was probably no more than a few minutes.

I stopped. There were no more explosions and suddenly Palmyra seemed very dark and very quiet and I felt very isolated.

'What are you doing?' the owner said urgently, turning to face me. 'We have to run. It's not safe here for you.'

'Where are we going?' I asked.

It was beginning to dawn on me that this man could be leading me into a trap. I didn't know him at all. I had only eaten at his café a few times: it was hardly enough of a bond for me to place my life in his hands. Yet if I didn't trust him, who else was there?

'Come, my brother is waiting for us, come,' he said.

Should I go, I thought? Who the hell was his brother? For all I knew his brother could be old one-eye or the giant from the café. Damned if I did and damned if I didn't. I reasoned, though, that this bloke had at least taken me away from the explosions, and that was a good thing. I decided to follow him.

After a few more minutes of running through the dark back streets of Palmyra we arrived at a black car. The driver, who had a cigarette clamped firmly in his mouth, gave us a slight nod and motioned for us to get in, which we did, still panting. He turned over the ignition and we pulled away slowly at very low revs. Whether he deliberately didn't turn the lights on to prevent us from being detected or they simply didn't work, I didn't know, but he was clearly being very cautious. This was certainly unusual in Syria, where 'cautious' and 'driving' were rare bedfellows.

After crawling along for ten minutes, we arrived outside a small apartment block and I was again instructed to follow the café owner. He led me up a staircase and into an apartment on the third floor.

Inside, a scene of absolute normality greeted me. A family sat around drinking tea and eating dates while watching TV.

It was like entering a different world. The driver came in with us, introducing himself as Mohammed. It turned out that, as well as being the brother of the café owner and thus another cousin of the bloke who owned my hotel, he was also the owner of the apartment.

After he'd sat me down and I'd been served with sweet tea, he tried to explain to me what had just gone on.

'The men in the café tonight were bad men,' he began. His brother nodded in agreement. 'They are from a group that wanted my brother to hand you to them.'

By 'hand me to them' he actually meant 'assist in my kidnapping'.

'But my brother is a good man and he refused.' The café owner smiled and nodded proudly. 'After the men left the café, they threatened my brother but he thought it was just words.'

I looked at the café owner and he nodded again.

'Then they told one of my friends that they were going to kill you. That's when I called my brother on the phone and told him to close the café and run.'

I distinctly remembered the café owner telling me there was 'no problem': it was a good job he'd listened to his brother.

'The explosions you heard were the grenades they threw at the café.' So these guys had been really serious. 'They didn't cause a lot of damage, though.'

I thanked Mohammed and his brother for saving me and then asked the obvious question: 'Why did they want me? I haven't done anything to cause trouble.'

Mohammed looked at me sympathetically and then said simply, 'My friend, you represent the west, their enemy, and they saw an opportunity. Don't let it worry you.'

I made a note to myself not to take a little thing like a targeted grenade attack personally in future.

Mohammed told me that it wouldn't be safe to go back to my hotel. He invited me to stay with his family for the night. His cousin, the hotel owner, would pack my belongings and bring them over (along with my bill) when he could. He also told me that I would need to leave Palmyra at first light, and that he would drive me back to Damascus.

The next morning at 5am, the hotel owner showed up with my belongings and my passport. I paid my bill and jumped into the car with Mohammed. He gave me a shemagh (scarf) to put over my head and advised me to put my sunglasses on too.

The drive out of town took us past the café and I could see that the metal shutter had taken much of the grenade blast. They'd need a new shutter but the building itself was largely undamaged. Without that shutter, though, and the assistance of the owner, there wouldn't have been much left of me.

I asked Mohammed whether his brother would be safe. He assured me that he was not the intended target, and that half of the discussion in the café had been about wanting to protect the owner rather than harm him. It wasn't in their interest to make enemies of the local population.

I was relieved. The last thing I wanted was for anyone to be put at risk just because of an association with me.

The car journey was a fascinating one as I learnt much from Mohammed about the region and the problems it faced. When we parted, I gave him all the money I had on me to give to his brother towards the cost of a new shutter.

IMPROVING THE ODDS

Having been the target of an attack myself, I know that threats can be real, and that is why I maintain my training and the skills required to keep myself safe while travelling overseas. This is something everyone should be doing, particularly if they are travelling to a region of high risk.

As a bare minimum you should take a travel-specific first aid course. The standard first aid at work courses are great for urban environments where you know there'll be an ambulance along in a few minutes and a couple of trained professionals with all their medical kit. If you're heading for a hostile environment overseas, however, you'll need a much more practical course; one that will enable you to deal with longer-term pre-hospital care. This could save not only your own life but also the lives of those around you.

If you are going to a region where there is a significant threat of kidnap or terrorist attacks, you would be an idiot, to put it bluntly, not to sign up for a hostile environment course. But do your research first. Cheapest is not necessarily best when it's your safety at stake and there are plenty of training providers out there who simply don't have the right knowledge, skills and experience to be training what is a highly specialised subject.

When preparing to go abroad, regularly check official government advice for the country you intend to visit and subscribe to their email alerts. Keep an eye on the news about the country in general and the region(s) you'll be visiting in particular. If trouble seems to be brewing, you may need to change your plans.

Once you arrive at your destination, be vigilant, particularly in public places that attract foreigners and westerners, such as hotels, restaurants, bars and beaches. Watch out for anything that looks suspicious. Anyone with bad intentions will give off warning signs in their body language or behaviour, whether they are a petty criminal or a terrorist. Don't ignore these signals and distance yourself from anyone behaving suspiciously. Many terrorist attacks are foiled by ordinary people spotting and reporting things that seem somehow out of place.

Identify 'safe' havens – predesignated places which you can head for in the event of an attack – making sure that there are alternative routes in and out. Notify all members of your team (or family) as to where these places are and practise how you're going to reach them. In the chaos of a real incident you may well get separated from the people you're with: rather than hanging around looking for colleagues or loved ones, make sure that everyone knows what to do and where to go in the event of an attack.

Think carefully about how you can blend into the crowd, particularly when you are visiting rural, out-of-town destinations.

Identify places along your route that might be useful in an emergency, such as police stations, hospitals and official buildings. Programme emergency numbers into your mobile and be sure to keep it charged at all times.

Be doubly discreet on social media about your plans and day-to-day exploits (see pages 57–59). Inform hotel staff, colleagues or friends about where you are going and when you intend to return.

WHAT TO DO IF IT ALL GOES WRONG

In the admittedly highly unlikely event that you are caught up in a terrorist situation, remember 'Run–Hide–Fight'. In some countries this is referred to as 'Run–Hide–Tell', but I use the 'fight' version in this book, as it may be your only option.

Your first instinct should be to run, to put as much time and distance as you can between the terrorists and yourself. Don't wait to collect your belongings, and don't stay in a crowd: terrorists tend to aim their fire at the highest density of people.

If for any reason you can't run; hide – and find the best hiding place you can, even if it's simply to conceal yourself behind a large object. But remember: if you can see an attacker, they can probably see you. Being out of sight, however, doesn't necessarily mean you are safe: bullets can pass through glass, some bricks, wood and lighter metals, depending on the calibre of the weapon and the thickness of the object you're hiding behind.

Lock doors, turn off lights and make sure that your mobile phone is switched off or on silent and non-vibrate mode. Don't move until you are absolutely convinced security forces have secured the scene. This could take hours.

Finally, if you can't run or hide, fight with every bone in your body. Then at least you have a chance of incapacitating your attacker and getting away. Improvise weapons from whatever is available and throw everything you can into your attack. This is not a time for holding back.

Once security forces are on scene, try to remain calm, keep your hands in clear view and follow their instructions quickly and quietly. Remember that their first objective will be to neutralise the threat rather than to treat casualties. Only once the scene is safe will the injured be dealt with. Don't be surprised if you are handled roughly by the security forces and make sure you comply with their instructions.

If you are caught up in an explosion inside a building and debris is falling round you, try to get under a sturdy table or desk. When the debris stops falling, leave the place as quickly as possible, watching out for areas that have been obviously weakened by the blast, such as floors and stairways. If there is smoke, keep low, crawling along the floor. Don't stop to retrieve personal possessions. Don't stand in front of windows, glass doors or other potential hazards.

If you find yourself trapped, if possible use a torch or smartphone light to signal your location to rescuers. Otherwise, tap on a wall or pipe. Shout only as a last resort, as raising your voice could cause you to inhale large volumes of dust. Similarly, avoid unnecessary movement so that you don't kick up dust particles. Cover your mouth and nose with anything you have to hand. Dense-weave cotton makes a good filter, so if all else fails, breathe through the material of your t-shirt.

TERRORISM SAFETY CHECKLIST

- If your instincts tell you something isn't right, move on, and report suspicious behaviour to the authorities as soon as possible. Trust your gut instinct and don't hang around.
- Move quickly. Most people who fall victim during an attack do so early on. This is either because they were close to the source of the attack when it started or because they subsequently hesitated or became immobilised. Find your nearest escape route as quickly as possible.
- Be aware that temporary restrictions on local and international travel may follow an attack, and this can make it difficult to leave the area. Alternatively, a total evacuation may be required. Follow the advice of local officials and security personnel.
- In the event of an attack, health and community resources will be stretched to the limit and it may be difficult to get the help you need right away. Stay calm and listen to the advice of local officials.
- Take note of your immediate surroundings and of the possibility of additional attacks. Listen to local TV and radio for information, check for injuries and, if you are able, administer first aid to yourself and/or others.
- Be aware that mobile phone networks are likely to be overwhelmed or even shut down after an attack, so you may not be able to communicate with the outside world. Try to get notification out as soon as you can. I was in Moscow during the 2010 Metro bombings and just managed to send a text to my client to say that the team were safe so that next of kin (including my own wife) could be informed. Minutes after I received the client's response, the mobile network crashed. It was two days before proper service was re-established.

CHAPTER ELEVEN

ESSENTIAL KIT

Packing for a big trip can be pretty daunting. While it's imperative that you have the right kit when travelling overseas, far too often I see people who err way too highly on the side of caution and pack everything including the kitchen sink. They are completely weighed down by their baggage and, not surprisingly, this can cast a real shadow over the trip.

Packing light requires careful thought as well as a fair amount of discipline. Don't fall into the trap of packing something because you 'might need it'. The chances are that the item will not make it out of your bag until you get back home.

Make sure that the clothes you pack are practical for your journey and fit for purpose. There is little point taking formal clothing if you are heading out on a trekking expedition. Remember to take practical items, such as a hat to protect your head from the sun and/or cold, and think about layers rather than packing your whole collection of sweaters and coats. Footwear is something that you don't want to compromise on – I always advocate doing your sightseeing in footwear that is both practical and comfortable. If you need to move quickly, trainers (sneakers) are far more effective than flip-flops or heels, so you'll also be able to explore for longer.

After years of travelling, I like to think that I've got packing down to a fine art. To keep clothing down to a minimum, I generally work on the rule of three: for each item I take one to wear, one for the wash and one clean one. Clearly, your individual requirements will be determined by the reason for your travels, but this is as good a starting point as any.

In addition, there are some items that I always travel with, and these are what I would consider to be essential kit for any journey, regardless of whether it's a two-day business trip or a two-month expedition. Obviously everyone has their own personal favourites, but listed on the next few pages are the bits of kit I regard as indispensable.

TRAVEL PACKING ESSENTIALS

1. HEAD TORCH
Whatever crisis situation you encounter, be it an aircraft emergency, a hotel fire, a natural disaster or merely a power cut, a head torch will always come in handy. As well as enabling you to see, it can also make you visible to others, whilst allowing your hands to remain free. However, if it's going to be of real use, you need to keep it close at hand with its batteries fully charged. For this reason I always carry a head torch in my day-bag and in my carry-on luggage on an aircraft.

2. DUCT TAPE
Duct tape is probably not an item high up on most people's packing list but it should be, because it has so many uses. I have used duct tape to provide a temporary fix to a radiator hose pipe on a jeep in Kenya, enabling us to get to the next town to get it repaired properly. I have also used it to help splint broken bones, repair tents, boots and broken windows, and even build shelters. It really is remarkable stuff and the one time you don't pack it you can guarantee you'll need it.

A big roll of duct tape is cumbersome and heavy so what I tend to do is to wind a smaller amount of it round an old plastic store card. This enables you to keep a significant supply of tape in a much more compact form. In fact, you can wrap duct tape around almost anything – a drink bottle, a pen, a walking pole, a bicycle frame if you are on a cycling trip or a paddle if you are a kayaker. You just need to make sure that you have it to hand when you need it.

3. FIRST AID KIT

A decent first aid kit is essential. Don't rely on the off-the-shelf kits from your local pharmacy or supermarket, as these just aren't designed for your particular trip and your personal health requirements. You're much better off spending some time putting together a personalised kit tailor-made for the trip you're taking and the environment you'll be in. If you are going to a location remote from medical facilities, think along the lines of longer-term, pre-hospital care. Make sure you include in your kit any medications and sanitary items you may need, as well as sterile 'giving kits' of needles, cannulas and syringes. Your first aid kit should be kept in your day-bag/carry-on luggage, but if you don't want them confiscated, remember to put any needles, scissors or blades in your hold luggage before you check in.

4. DOOR STOPPER

This is possibly one of the most simple yet effective security devices available for the traveller: simply wedge it under the door of your accommodation for added in-room security. Stoppers can be remarkably cheap – you could even make a wooden wedge yourself. In fact, in my experience the best door stoppers have been homemade. Alternatively, there are some really fancy versions available from retailers. Some even come fitted with alarms so that if they are displaced a loud sound is emitted. This means that, even if you're sound asleep, you will be alerted to the fact that someone is trying to get into your room. My only word of caution with the more expensive kind of door stopper is that, the more moving parts or electronic components there are, the more can go wrong. I prefer to keep things as simple as possible.

5. MOBILE PHONE

Smartphones are great and these days most people have one. However, they are also high-value items and thus extremely desirable to criminals. Also, unless you want to pay roaming charges, they are of limited use when you travel in many countries. That's why I always carry a cheap but robust mobile phone when I travel, with nothing more fancy than text and phone call capability. I've found that the less complicated phones are often the most reliable and have a longer battery life, so you're not looking for a charger every five minutes. Also, if you do get robbed, they're easier and cheaper to replace.

When I get to my destination, I purchase a local network sim card and therefore only pay local rates for in-country calls and texts. I also make sure to plan ahead and store all the important numbers I might need for that particular trip. These would include any local contacts, my hotel, the emergency services, the embassy or consulate, and emergency contacts back home.

6. DUMMY WALLET/PURSE

Hopefully, if you implement the personal security precautions advocated in this book, you will avoid becoming a victim of crime. However, if you are robbed, it is better to hand over a dummy wallet or purse that contains items of low or no value rather than losing vital documents, cards and money. As I mentioned in chapter 4, criminals rarely hang around to check the contents of a bag or wallet they steal: they want to get away as soon as they can. By the time they find out that they've been duped, hopefully you'll be in a place of safety with your real valuables secure.

7. SARONG

Strangely enough, I have found a sarong to be a very handy piece of travel kit. Yes, you can use it as a skirt, but it can also be used as a towel, a headdress (especially in Muslim countries), a sheet, a wrap, a sack, a scarf and a screen. I have also used a sarong as a sling for a broken arm, and I'm sure there are more uses that I have yet to discover. It's a versatile piece of kit that's lightweight and packs down to almost nothing.

8. MULTI-PURPOSE TOOL

Multi-purpose tools are sold under various brand names and include different combinations of tools. They can include pliers, screwdrivers of different kinds, saws, knife blades, wire cutters, diamond-coated files, bottle and tin openers, scissors, even rulers, all in one small object. In fact, they can offer just about everything you might need to mend, make, build, repair and adapt while you are on your travels. Some people prefer the more traditional Swiss Army knife, which include tweezers, corkscrews and toothpicks as well as the various blades: it's a matter of personal choice. Take what suits your travel plans best. Just don't pack it in your hand luggage when you're flying or it will be confiscated at the airport, and these tools don't come cheap.

9. ANTISEPTIC HAND WASH

Standards of hygiene vary greatly around the world and we can therefore be at great risk of picking up unwelcome germs when we travel. Good personal hygiene habits are an excellent way to help avoid health problems, and so I always carry a decent supply of antiseptic hand wash. I use this regularly myself, especially after going to the toilet and before handling food, and I also make a point of encouraging others to do the same, sharing my own supplies if necessary. This travel essential doesn't have to be a bulky addition to your luggage and most places (including airports) sell it in handy 50ml bottles. If you're carrying it in your hand luggage, though, remember that more than 100ml will again get confiscated. One note of caution: while most brands claim to kill 99.9 per cent of all bacteria, it's not a cure-all: you should still watch out for hygiene issues in all aspects of your travel, especially when deciding what and where to eat and drink.

10. MULTI-PLUG ADAPTOR

Our reliance on electronic appliances means that the ability to charge gadgets has become an essential aspect of travel. Many of the devices that require a charger are, in fact, the very things we often rely on to keep us safe, such as phones (mobile and satellite), radios, GPS (sat-nav), laptops and tablets. Therefore, make sure that you have the right adaptor for charging your devices, or else in an emergency they will be totally useless. Electricity sockets vary greatly from country to country, so if you're travelling through a number of different places, a multi-plug adaptor will save you carrying lots of different ones. Be sure that you keep your devices charged: in some regions power outages are frequent and you never know when there's going to be a power cut.

11. VAGABAND TRAVELLERS ID

I test a lot of travel safety kits and I consider it a perk of my job. Much of it is gimmicky or relies on electricity or technology to function. I prefer simple equipment that is robust, tech-free and serves a genuine purpose. Vagaband is the original travellers' safety wristband. It provides the clearest, simplest and easiest way to make sure that your most important medical, insurance and personal details are recorded and with you. With just a pencil, new information can be added or edited at any time, meaning that whatever is written in the band is always relevant, accurate and up-to-date. The bands are waterproof and tear resistant, as well as being resistant to high temperatures, sunscreens and insect repellents. So, if you get into trouble, even if you're unconscious, all your vital information is contained on your Vagaband.

12. WATER-TO-GO

Water-To-Go is a unique water filtration system. It protects you by removing all bad stuff from your water, while keeping good stuff like minerals. It is ideal for overseas travel as you can fill up from almost any water source and it will even filter out nasties like Weil's disease, Giardia, Cryptosporidium and E. coli, as well as viruses. It is lightweight and each filter works for about 200 litres of water, which means it's also cost effective and good for the environment.

13. SAFE HARNESS

This truly is a lifesaving piece of kit, particularly for those travelling in the more remote and poorer regions of the world where vehicle safety standards are lower than we would expect at home. The Safe Harness System is a personal safety device that is easily installed on a coach-style seat by placing it over the seat back and sliding it down to the seat cushion. It's then secured in place by pulling on the belt, which is kept taught because of a specially designed tension device. The Safe Harness System takes the shape of a standard lap belt and provides the passenger with an effective safety device. It comes in a neat and easy-to-store pouch, so won't take up much room in your luggage.

14. PERSONAL ALARM

Personal attack alarms have been on the market for a while now, but they are a good way of alerting others that you are in danger and giving the element of surprise, even if it's just enough for you to put time and distance between you and a potential attacker. They are particularly useful in places like hostels, where you are sharing rooms with strangers. They are also very cheap, so you can afford to take a back up. Go for one that kicks out at least 140 decibels.

15. TACTICAL FLASHLIGHT

A tactical flashlight is different from your head torch as it is designed to give off much brighter light. They are particularly useful if walking in dark areas, or in your accommodation at night.

These things give off seriously bright light and most offer between 800 and 1,000 lumens of light output. That is going to temporarily stop anyone from doing what they're doing, affecting their night-vision, allowing you to take evasive action to get away. Most are made from aircraft-grade aluminium, making them very strong if you ever found yourself in a 'run–hide–fight' situation. Some also have an SOS Morse code function, which you can use in the case of getting lost or caught in an accommodation fire or natural disaster to alert the rescue services of your location.

ESSENTIAL KIT CHECKLIST

- Think about the type of luggage you buy. It's a fallacy that designer luggage will secure you an upgrade from an airline: instead, it may very well make you a prime target for a thief.
- Whether you are travelling for two weeks or two months, your luggage should be pretty much the same. You can wash your clothes and when you run out of toiletries you can easily replace them by buying them as you go along.
- If you worry you are taking too much, you probably are. Remember, you walk with your luggage a lot more than you think. If in doubt, practise walking around with it for a while. If you're staggering about, thin it out!
- Packing light isn't just about reducing the strain. There is nothing that marks you out more as a tourist than too much luggage. With one light bag you are more mobile and in control. Remember, there are only two sorts of traveller: those who pack light and those who wish they had.
- Never put in your luggage anything you'd really hate to lose.
- Suitcases and backpacks are easily parted from their luggage labels: always put a second label somewhere accessible.
- Try not to check in at the very last minute: while *you* may make it on to the flight, your luggage may not.

APPENDIX

There are numerous useful travel safety websites available that will be vital when you are planning and preparing for your next trip. These resources are an excellent place to start and will give you an edge when thinking about your own safety and security, whether you're travelling on business, on a gap year, or going on holiday.

- Obtaining official government advice on the regions you are planning to travel to is a vital first step, not least of all because it could affect your insurance policy. Many insurers don't cover people travelling to areas that your government advises against. However, don't just rely on one source. I find the following give me a good overview of what different governments are saying about a country or region and, trust me, they do vary:
  - » The British Foreign & Commonwealth Office (FCO) Travel Advice: https://www.gov.uk/foreign-travel-advice
  - » The Australian Government Smart Traveller website is excellent and one I always look at before I set off: http://smartraveller.gov.au/Pages/default.aspx
  - » OSAC (Overseas Security Advisory Council) works with the US State Department to safeguard the interests of Americans operating overseas and is another great resource: https://www.osac.gov/Pages/Home.aspx
- The Aviation Safety Network has a comprehensive database of aircraft-related incidents. It also allows you to look at the safety

record of just about every airline in the world, allowing you to make an informed decision as to who you fly with: https://aviation-safety.net

- Natural disasters can strike with little or no warning, so knowing the latest advice on what to do if you are caught in one is an essential part of your preparation. For me, the New Zealand government site Get Ready Get Thru covers just about everything you need to know to prepare yourself for a natural disaster: http://www.getthru.govt.nz

- Getting the right medical advice before you set off is not only essential for your health, but also key to you having a positive travel experience. There are a couple of resources I use to check the latest information on travel health risks:
  » The National Travel Health Network and Centre (NaTHNaC) is the UK Health Department's website and has loads of useful travel medical advice: https://travelhealthpro.org.uk
  » The other site I use is CDC (Centers for Disease Control and Prevention), which is the US equivalent of NaTHNaC, but also contains advice on emergency preparedness: https://www.cdc.gov

- For anything to do with water safety, make sure you check on the Royal National Lifeboat Institution (RNLI) website and in particular their Respect the Water campaign. The website has expert advice for just about any water-based activity: https://rnli.org

- Nowadays there's lots of official advice about what to do if you're unfortunate enough to get caught up in a terrorist attack. The UK government's Action Counters Terrorism (ACT) website has lots of useful information: https://act.campaign.gov.uk

- Getting the right training is also important, so you might want to consider taking courses to help keep you safe. My own company offers all manner of travel safety courses from First Aid all the way through to operating in hostile environments: http://www.lflglobalrisk.com/courses/

- Businesses looking to keep their staff safe when travelling should consider joining the Travel Risk & Incident Prevention (TRIP) Group™. This is a group made up of risk management professionals dedicated to finding solutions to the challenges of travel safety: https://thetripgroup.com

AFTERWORD

The stories in this book represent a small but hopefully compelling snapshot of some of my adventures around the world. I have shared them here, along with the lessons I have learnt, to highlight some of the more dangerous aspects of travel, but also how to mitigate those dangers. As I hope I have amply demonstrated, things can and do go wrong, often when you least expect them to.

I do feel, though, that these tales should be put into context: I have been travelling in one capacity or another since I was eight months old, and while my work has often taken me to some dangerous places, by far the vast majority of my travels have been trouble-free.

There is not a single incident that I have recounted here that has made me reconsider my desire to travel. Every time I get home, even after the most challenging trips, I am always thinking about and planning for the next adventure. Travel has allowed me to meet some remarkable people and to visit some incredible places, and I have enjoyed all my trips, even when things didn't go quite as I expected.

I sincerely hope this proves to be true for anyone who reads this book. Nevertheless, it is important to bear in mind that there are dangers out there and people who would see harm come to travellers. It is therefore essential that you know the potential risks, as this will greatly improve your chances of avoiding them. But you shouldn't let the possible pitfalls put you off and by travelling with your eyes open to them, you will increase your confidence and your chances of having an enjoyable and memorable experience.

I have travelled to more than 80 countries and hopefully that number will continue to increase, but each time I set out I go through the same routine as if for the first time. It can be very dangerous to take things for granted: I have seen and heard of many people who dropped their guard because they were familiar with a certain place or route, only to come unstuck because of their complacency.

When I was a soldier there was a phrase that was repeated and repeated until it was drilled into our subconscious. It was known as the seven Ps: 'Proper planning and preparation prevents piss-poor performance.' It's a phrase that has stuck with me and that comes back time and time again as I set out on each adventure.

One of the Founding Fathers of the United States, Benjamin Franklin, provided a perhaps better-known (and more polite) version: 'By failing to prepare, you are preparing to fail.' Both reflect the same sentiment: never underestimate the benefits gained from proper preparation.

Reflect on this before each trip, take note of the advice in this book and you'll do just fine. In other words, remember to keep looking for lemons. Make sure you deal with them effectively when they occur and don't let them build up into something you can't handle. Remember, never push a bad position, it will only get worse. I'm a great believer that it's the little things that make a huge difference and in this book I have provided you with plenty of little travel safety tips. Added together, the advice contained in the book provides the reader with a wealth of knowledge that, when implemented, will make a fundamental difference to how you view your safety, security and wellbeing when travelling.

There is nothing in life quite like travel for enhancing your knowledge and broadening your horizons. It's probably why so many of us get bitten by the travel bug and keep going back for more.

So, what are you waiting for? Get planning for your next adventure, get off the beaten track and explore this incredible planet: there's a whole wide world out there to discover.

Good luck and safe travels.

ACKNOWLEDGEMENTS

There are so many people who have played a part in the writing of this book. My parents, Phil and Pam, have continually given their support, despite all I have put them through. And trust me, that's more than any parent should endure in one lifetime. They have always encouraged me to go out and live life to the full, although there may have been times when their definition of 'full' was somewhat different from mine.

As we were growing up, my brother Mike was responsible for most of the trouble I got into, but he was also the person I looked up to. I have him to thank for teaching me how to 'manage' risk in those early years.

This book would never have happened without the love and support of my amazing wife, Nicky. She makes me laugh when the going gets tough and is the voice of reason when I can't see the wood for the trees. Not only is she my wife but she's also my confidant and best friend. I couldn't have done it without her. Thank you.

Travelling to remote areas can sometimes be a dangerous affair, and you therefore need to choose the right travel companion. For me there is none better than my good friend Maverick. He and I have shared many a sticky situation as well as many a laugh. He has been a constant reminder for me of why we travel and why we need to continually push boundaries.

There are others who have supported me in this endeavour, even if they don't realise it. Sean Lambourne has always been a great friend and full of good advice when I needed it most. It was also he who provided the voucher for the hotel in Dakar (see page 121).

Thanks to Caroline Rogan, who was so often there with me; Sir Ranulph Fiennes, who has been unfailingly generous in his support and advice; Joyce Burnett for all her help; Kim Cassello, Alana Jones, Anne Ogilvie and Nigel Winser, who have all at some stage shared the dubious pleasure of being my boss and who also share my passion for making travel safer; Professor David Warrell and Dr Matt Ladbrook, who have always provided me with sage medical advice and are the best expedition doctors I know, and Sheena Browne from whom I have learnt so much; Shane Winser who has led the way in expedition safety and who is someone I have often turned to for advice; and Rose Youd, whose literary fine-tuning is much appreciated.

I would also like to thank Miles and Ava Shacklady for providing up-to-date advice and an insight into the travel challenges faced by young people; Joel Whittaker, who knows more than anyone should on travelling in hostile regions; and Sue Williams QPM and Blue Cole for their expertise in kidnap awareness and avoidance.

INDEX

First published in the United Kingdom in 2018 by

Portico
43 Great Ormond Street
London
WC1N 3HZ

An imprint of Pavilion Books Company Ltd.

Design: Tatiana Losinska and Tokiko Morishima

ISBN 978-1-84165-792-9

A CIP catalogue record for this book is available from the British Library.

Printed and bound by CPI Group UK Ltd.

This book can be ordered direct from the publisher at www.pavilionbooks.com